The Fall of Fortresses

Other Books by Elmer Bendiner

THE BOWERY MAN

A TIME FOR ANGELS
The Tragicomic History of the League of Nations

THE VIRGIN DIPLOMATS

THE FALL OF FORTRESSES

A Personal Account of the Most
Daring—and Deadly—American
Air Battles of World War II

By

Elmer Bendiner

G. P. Putnam's Sons
New York

Library of Congress Cataloging in Publication Data

Bendiner, Elmer.
  The fall of fortresses.

  1. Schweinfurt, Ger.—Bombardment, 1943—Personal
narratives, American. 2. Bendiner, Elmer. 3. World
War, 1939-1945—Aerial operations, American. I. Title.
D757.9.S35B46   1980   940.54'21   79-24194
ISBN 0-399-12372-5

Printed in the United States of America

To Esther, Jessica, Winnie, Paul, and Gabrielle

1

It is now thirty-five years since I climbed a fence to pick a poppy in an English meadow on which lay the mists of an August morning. The memory of that poppy prompts some questions that are urgent now though they did not seem even relevant thirty-five years ago.

Then it was enough to be there—good enough or bad enough, depending on how one chose to play the soldier. It did not seem important to know the details of the plan that set me down in such a place at such an hour to be told that I was to be one of those who on that day— August 17, 1943—were to strike the blow that would destroy Hitler and end the war.

An ordinary young man is not often told that what he and a few others may do between breakfast and dinner will change the course of world history. Confronted now with so awesome a responsibility, I would shudder. But thirty-five years ago it was quite in order to believe that the world could be undone and reborn in the twinkling of

9

an eye and that I was to be an agent of that cataclysmic revolution. It was an age—my age, perhaps—when the world each morning stood on the brink of catastrophe or redemption.

As I recall, neither I nor anyone else in the briefing room expressed more than the mildest surprise at the announcement that this day our little band of flying brothers would win the war. We were preoccupied with a more modest objective, survival.

It was plain that many of us would not survive that August day. The Brass would not have laid such solemn stress on our importance unless a good many of us were unlikely to hear the applause afterward. Our suspicions were confirmed by the very length of red woolen yarn that ran across a brightly colored map of western Europe. At our briefings targets were ritually greeted with groans of mock fear to mask the real fear. This time when the intelligence captain parted the blackout curtains to reveal the yarn's astonishing reach, the groans were noisier, the clowning more frenzied.

The formidable red line began at an assembly point over the Wash, that marshy bay that notches the east coast of England in Lincolnshire. From there it ran south to the Essex coast and left England at Clacton-on-Sea. It headed across the Channel to the Dutch islands of Walcheren, South Beveland and Schouwen, where, it was noted, there would be moderate flak. (I recalled from earlier flights the dull gleam of rooftops on those flat, hazed islands. I envisioned the black puffs that always preceded the shocks like foamy swells of a choppy sea. I heard again the *ping* of shrapnel.)

The string ran over Holland, promising a glimpse of the delicate rectilinear patterns of canals. Then, passing north and east of Antwerp, the red line would take us over Aachen at the German border, where our fighter escort of Spitfires and Thunderbolts would have to turn back and leave all of Germany to us or us to the Germans. The crimson wool shot like an arrow past the snakelike bends of the Mosel to the Rhine at Wiesbaden, then turned sharply east and headed over the Main River, which should serve as an unmistakable checkpoint. (I had no doubt that the Main when seen from 26,000 feet would be a blue corkscrew because I had found that if one travels at sufficient altitude the world becomes abstract until it resembles, in color, form and texture, the linen flying maps of the RAF.) At Würzburg the line pivoted ninety degrees and headed north to a pin that punctured Germany at a place called Schweinfurt.

It was an exhausting piece of wool to contemplate, but I was prepared to accept it. I sat there watching the men in my crew, my squadron. I knew that some of them (I did not dare to wonder which) would that day die. Still, I was certain that morning as on other mornings that I would return. No matter that even those who were in fact about to die were as certain as I of their own survival.

I would survive that woolen thread, but only if I followed my private ritual, only if I went and found a poppy to put in my buttonhole. I had worn poppies before and survived. I am a reasonable man, but in matters of life and death I do not exclude talismans simply because they are magical and absurd.

Besides, I fancied the poppy as a flower. Its colors are strong and its texture is delicate. It reminds me of those Japanese paper flowers which, when dropped into water, unfold to reveal a parasol or a flag. My poppy, immersed in my aging civilian mind, conjures up grisly surprises— a man with his head blown off along with his turret, or

11

the image of twenty-six dead children in a city I have bombed. And there are also great and foolish splendors that unfold. I am embarrassed to admit that the palpable presence of death can offer such intoxicating attractions, but that is the perverse nature of my war and of flying.

On that August morning in 1943, however, the poppy was no plaything but my highly personal assurance of survival. With it I could go to Schweinfurt and probably come back. It was as if I had suspended all rational disciplined skepticism for the duration.

Obviously I had been shaped with some care. To an extent I would scarcely have thought possible I had given myself up to those who with undeniable craftsmanship had created a soldier out of my common civilian clay. However I might rage at the absurdity, stupidity, even occasional malevolence of those who made me, I grudgingly admitted that they had pulled off a most unlikely miracle. I did more or less what I was designed to do. And I refrained from doing what was not in the operating manual that covered my particular mechanism.

I was not geared, for example, to ask very many questions and certainly not that most incapacitating of interrogatories: why? Yet here was Major Rip Rohr answering the question that had not been asked: Why Schweinfurt? He was a spry little foxlike man, with a cowlick hanging over his black eyes, a peppery little man who always seemed to be dancing on tiptoes like a bantam boxer, clamoring to fly on every mission, reaching for glory in a way that was quite extraordinary for a soldier.

It seemed preposterously un-Army for the major to be confiding in us. We had never known precisely why we went on other excursions. We had no need to know why now. We were not to vote on whether his explanation was convincing, whether the mission was worth the risk, whether we should not consider the pros and cons of the matter at greater length.

If he had said that we were going to bomb Schweinfurt for the exercise, we would have grumbled but we would have gone. His explanation was interesting, of course. But his giving it was ominous because it was a departure from custom. Any departure—even the most reasonable—from established practice before a battle seems to be inviting disaster. It would have been better for Rip to have kept to his customary speech. It would have been safer if he had closed with the ritualistic sendoff: "Good luck, good hunting and . . . G-o-o-d-b-y-e." Instead, the major stood at the lectern, with schoolmaster's pointer in hand, and read from notes. The target was not the town of Schweinfurt.

(We Americans never aimed at towns. General Ira C. Eaker, commanding the Eighth Air Force, had summed up our American approach: "We must never allow the record of this war to convict us of throwing the strategic bomber at the man in the street.")

Not Schweinfurt, then, but Kugelfischer & Co. was our prime target, and for subsidiary targets there were the Vereingte Kugellager Fabrik (a plant the Nazis had expropriated from its Swedish owners), the Deutsche Star Kugelhalter and the factories of Fichterl & Sachs Co. All were stretched along the winding Regnitz River. They made ball bearings which, we were told, were absolutely vital to the German war machine, needed to ease the friction of clashing parts.

The factories at Schweinfurt supplied fifty-eight percent (some said seventy-six percent) of the ball bearings used in German industry. With these plants out of commission German production and transport would be cut back. The tanks on the Russian front would be used up and there would be no replacements. The Luftwaffe would be grounded. Allied infantry need not invade Europe; they would parade through it.

"We've got 'em by the balls," said a gunner.

Rip Rohr's speech was not eloquent. It was delivered in the staccato of a sergeant reading a roster by flashlight in a shivering dawn. But would it have mattered if Laurence Olivier had played the part? I think not. The script was at fault. Shakespeare put into the mouth of Henry V at Agincourt not a sober estimate of the strategic importance of the castle of Harfleur but a magnificent war cry calculated to make a soldier drunk with the sense of his own shining honor.

Actually I doubt that such a speech would have worked with us. We would have mistrusted it, I think. We preferred to go to battle with the wry smile of inarticulate cinematic cowboys. In any case, soldiers— whether at Agincourt or Schweinfurt—did not ask why. Throughout our training we had sung the quintessential soldier's song, "We're here because we're here because we're here because we're here."

Why, then, did our superiors on Schweinfurt morning violate our innocence with information? I savored the importance of the occasion though I did not quite believe it. There was little talk of it when we jumped off the truck at the hardstand where *Tondelayo* waited. We gathered under her wing and tried to see through the mists to the end of the runway. The pale sun scarcely seemed strong enough to dry the dew on the flower I had fastened in my buttonhole. We did not know whether what we had been told was true. We did not much care. We knew that many of us would die, and still we wanted the battle to begin. We prayed that the mission would not be scrubbed.

Though a scrubbed mission guarantees another day of life, I cannot recall a single scrub that was ever cheered. I remember only the dark, tired looks, the helmets hurled across the beds, the suffocating cloud of frustration sticking in the throat like a sour regurgitation, a sense of total waste.

On that August morning messages came flying from the tower postponing takeoff time once, then a second time and a third time while rumor played upon our nerves like the whine of a dog when the air is stifling and one yearns to feel the wind rise. We wanted to hear the high-pitched sound of the warmup generators. We lusted for the explosive roar of the propellers. We were tuned and ready. Yet we waited.

To tell the story of Schweinfurt solely from the vantage point of those young men sitting under *Tondelayo's* wing on a soggy airfield would be like describing the battle of Waterloo as seen by one man who plunged a bayonet into the belly of another and perhaps another after that. It would be valid, though it might look more like murder than war. The limitations of a soldier's view of battle were neatly described by A. W. Kinglake, who wrote of an earlier war:

> In so far as the battlefield presented itself to the bare eyesight of men, it had no entirety, no length, no breadth, no depth, no size, no shape, and was made up of nothing except small numberless circlets commensurate with such ranges of vision as the mist might allow at each spot . . . in such conditions, each separate gathering of English soldiery went on fighting its own little battle in happy and advantageous ignorance of the general state of the

action; nay, even very often in ignorance that any great conflict was raging.

I am no longer that young man under *Tondelayo*'s wing and I have looked beyond the circlet of our battle. My questions are not political in the narrow sense, for I have never been in doubt about the necessity of that particular war. It was perhaps the nearest approach to Armageddon that we have seen or shall ever see. It would be something akin to blasphemy to talk that struggle down from its high tragedy and make it seem like a brawl in a marketplace.

The questions I have are simple, though they may produce a chain reaction of unforeseeable dimensions.

I want to know, for example, how we of *Tondelayo* got to Schweinfurt in the first place. Who thought the destruction of the Kugelfischer Werke worth all those lives—some 1,200 American airmen in the first two raids, and numberless Germans? What spies, what researchers burrowing in what libraries unearthed the statistics that sent us off to scatter our burning planes and bodies all over Europe? And did we win or lose?

2

The archives suggest that the genesis of the battle of Schweinfurt was absurdly accidental. Apparently the city was first nominated as a high-priority target during an informal party in wartime Washington. It was December 20, 1942, and the gathering was at the home of the Swedish minister. Among the guests were the minister's son-in-law, Sexton Wolmar, and a colonel of Army Air Forces Intelligence, Guido Perera.

As Colonel Perera was later to describe that evening in a formal report, he and Mr. Wolmar were discussing trivia as befitted the occasion when the conversation took a sharp turn. It seemed that the very suddenness with which Wolmar changed his tone and subject matter underscored the significance of what he had to say.

"I see that you are now in the Air Corps," Wolmar told the colonel, then added abruptly, "Why doesn't the Air Corps knock out the ball-bearings plants at Schweinfurt? Germany couldn't get along without them."

If Colonel Perera had been no more than a desk officer and Mr. Wolmar no more than an industrialist playing at armchair strategy to pass the time, their conversation would not have been recorded in a formal report preserved in the archives of the Air Force. And perhaps we would not have gone off to Schweinfurt on a mission so extravagantly billed.

What freighted Mr. Wolmar's question with consequence was the fact that he was a vice-president of the American subsidiary of S.K.F., the company that was producing much of America's supply of ball bearings. And Colonel Perera had just been assigned to a committee that was to nominate German targets for our force of bombers then struggling to be born amid a clamor of competing demands, plans and objectives. Perera valued the source of the suggestion and was in a position to elaborate and refine it so that in time it might materialize as the end point of a ball of yarn.

That same casual sort of happenstance seems to have attended Colonel Perera's appointment to the Committee of Operations Analysts (COA), organized to probe for cracks in the German armor.

As I study the archives now, so many years after the event, I find it hard to believe that affairs of such moment could be brought about with the seeming mindlessness of a collision of molecules moving at random.

Yet such is the inescapable impression left by Colonel Perera's report in which he described the formation of the COA seventeen days before the party at the Swedish minister's. He wrote, with elaborate self-deprecation, that he had been "occupying a desk" in the office of General Byron E. Gates, assistant chief of air staff, management control, on December 3, 1942, when General Muir S. Fairchild, director of military requirements of the Army Air Forces, made what is described as "an informal call" upon General Gates. Merely because Colonel Perera happened to be in General Gates's office, he said, he was included in the conversation. One is left with the impression that anyone who happened to be at that desk at that time might have ended up picking targets for the U.S. Army Air Forces.

General Fairchild, according to the colonel, went from shop talk of no consequence to complaints about the inadequate presentation of Air Forces matters to the Joint Chiefs of Staff. Such disappointing performance was inevitable, the General went on in what appears to have been a soliloquy, because officers involved in daily routines were unable to work on solutions for such problems as those that beset the concept of strategic bombing.

"He also pointed out," Perera noted, "that this type of activity was one for which a regular army career did not necessarily prepare an officer."

It so happened that Perera was not a career officer and that he had just written a study of organizational problems in the Army, the Navy and the Air Forces, which General Fairchild had just happened to read.

General Gates, apparently working on cue, put Perera and another officer at the disposal of General Fairchild, whereupon the General turned to Perera and said, "All right, I have a job for you. How can Germany be so damaged by an air attack that an invasion of the Continent may be made possible within a relatively short time, say one year?"

That, no doubt, was one of the questions that had been put to General Fairchild when he was appointed to the freshly formed Joint Strategic Survey Committee, and as a trained executive he set out to hire someone to provide the answer.

General Fairchild, who propounded the fateful question to Colonel Perera, was not merely a career officer looking for talent. General Fairchild embodied a venerable faith complete with holy mission, prophets and martyrs. Its earliest visionaries had beheld the truth in the midst of World War I. They and their disciples had been driven underground, and only now, when their ancient prophecies were about to be fulfilled, were they emerging from the shadows.

In 1932—ten years earlier—General Fairchild had directed a survey of strategic-bombardment capabilities. Since there was no enemy on the horizon in that year, or at least none that could be publicly described as potential bomb targets, Fairchild picked apart the American economy to show how any industrial state could be defeated by strategic bombing, properly directed to critical areas, industrial bottlenecks and vital centers.

That this could be done was a cardinal tenet of the founders of military aviation. Fairchild, then a colonel, was attempting—with no backing, much hostility and few resources—to follow their wisdom and proclaim their strength. In the thirties he did this at the Air Corps Tactical School at Maxwell Field, Alabama, a seminary and a temple for the glory of air power.

Just as the Second World War had its political roots in the First, so did the concept that was to be tested on Schweinfurt morning. The battle we were to fight that day was meant to be the vindication of the concept of strategic bombing. The target was to be bombed not to assist the movement of ground troops or in conjunction with an attack from the sea. It was a mission to be

performed by flyers alone, and it was to be decisive.
Indeed, it was the sort of vision that would establish the
Air Forces as the senior independent service in modern
warfare to which the older branches must yield all rights
of precedence.

This was the theory that had evolved out of the
dogfights of tiny biplanes in 1917 and 1918. We of
Tondelayo's crew were charged with proving the merits
of a concept hatched before most of us were born. Yet not
only was our strategy based on the thinking of those
early flying soldiers, but some of the high priests of their
creed were now our commanders, coming into their
belated prime. They were going to use us to prove their
point, however unconvinced or even uninterested we
were. I do not suggest that this was in any way
reprehensible. Sergeants and lieutenants are meant to
prove or disprove with their bodies the theories of
strategists.

I was nine years old in 1925 when the gallant,
flamboyant General Billy Mitchell was court-martialed.
I doubt that it made a great impression on me. I do not
remember it being mentioned at the dinner table, not
even by my grandfather, who was the most politically
aware member of my family because President
McKinley had once shaken his hand and left him
everlastingly Republican.

Billy Mitchell, ace of the late great war, who adorned
the rotogravure pages in cape, Cordovan boots and
British pinks, the American champion against the Teu-
tonic Knights of Richthofen's Flying Circus, had been in
the Army for twenty-one years. He had seen service in
the Philippines and China. He had been the first American to fly over enemy lines and in the battle of St.
Mihiel commanded 1,500 aircraft. He had come home

convinced that the Germans had shrewdly saved their army and the mystique of military glory by premature surrender, and that it would be only a matter of time before the war would have to be resumed. Next time, he told everyone who would listen, the war would be decided in the air by airmen. Inevitably planes would bomb not only armies but factories and cities. Engines of war would leap oceans and mountains. There would be no defense.

To inaugurate a new era of warfare required a new military service. To give that specialty its proper priority and to endow it with a romantic aura to make up for its novelty required either the compliance or the humiliation of the crusty old chiefs who held the purse strings. These men were not compliant, and Billy Mitchell was prepared to humiliate them.

Sporting his decorations—French as well as American—he came home from the war talking volubly and colorfully enough to make good copy. "The General Staff knows as much about air as a hog does about skating," he told the newspapers. "Armies and navies are no longer capable of enunciating or putting into effect the complete military policy for a country. The voice of the air must be listened to in all councils with equal force. . . . A standing army . . . [has] stood too long."

He proved that the day of the battleship was over and confounded the admirals by bombing a defunct battle queen to the bottom of the sea. It must be admitted. though, that his plane took an inordinate amount of time to do the job—some four or five hours—and in actual combat might have been blown out of the sky in the process, but that scarcely mattered. The admirals, who regarded the airplane as no more than an extension of the telescope, were momentarily upset and finally contrived another demonstration, designed to prove that airborne bombs inevitably fall wide of their target and are therefore no threat whatever to a well-run navy. Navy Under Secretary Franklin Delano Roosevelt declared, "It is highly unlikely that an airplane or a fleet of them could ever successfully attack a fleet of navy vessels under battle conditions."

It did not matter that Mitchell was not always meticulous as to the details of his prophecy. Even a divinely inspired prophet could not be expected to describe every mole on the face of an apocalyptic horseman. He carried in his mind's eye a vision of the next war and perhaps of the war after that. He described an "aerial torpedo . . . an instrument that goes through the air . . . similar to the way a water torpedo goes through the water, that is, an airplane with gyroscopic controls, and can be controlled by radio, with the object of hitting targets at a long distance."

He gave it as the unanimous opinion of knowledgeable airmen "that a future contest between nations would be preceded by two things: intensive action of submarines across the sea and air attack on the nerve centers of the hostile states so as to eliminate the will to fight." He foresaw the inevitable next war as "an elimination probably of the cannon fodder systems of the nations in arms as it has been practiced for the last two or three hundred years."

He shared the notion, common among flyers, that war is too heroic an enterprise to be vulgarized by mass participation. It was to be left to knights with parachute-silk scarves flung in careless grace about their necks.

Now—after so many wars in which gigantic planes have poured so much death upon so many towns, desolated so many homes and defoliated so many fields, often to obscure and inconclusive ends, now when one of the doomsdays most frequently prophesied envisions total annihilation by flying engines guided by moles in snug subterranean shelters—now Billy Mitchell's dream of a chivalric technology seems no more than a child's faith in the fundamental goodness of dragons.

But in the early twenties, after the buckets of blood and the spectacle of lice scurrying from corpses to more succulent flesh in the muck of the trenches, there were obvious attractions in another form of combat that would be fought alone with death in a blue empyrean. It was at least a clean way to settle an argument. The belief in air war was part of a faith in modernity. It was a time when painters saw glories in galvanized steel pipes, angular tubing and belching chimneys. Billy Mitchell romanticized the airplane in the way that Futurists romanticized chrome and social realists romanticized proletarians and Wilsonians romanticized universal parliaments.

Billy Mitchell spoke to America as Giulio Douhet spoke to Europe. That general had wrung from history the preposterous conclusion that it was his native Italy that had led the Allies to victory in the First World War. With a similar disdain of prosaic fact he began his book *The Command of the Air* by clearing away all hope of lasting peace so that there would be no alternative to his vision of the coming war. "Aeronautics opened up to men a new field of action, the field of the air," he wrote. "In so doing, it of necessity created a new battlefield; for wherever two men meet, conflict is inevitable."

In this view of the human potential for peace Douhet prefigured the position taken by Mussolini, his follower who became his leader. During his metamorphosis from Socialist to Fascist Mussolini wrote that "brotherhood is a fable which men listen to during the bivouac and the truce."

Douhet summed up the doctrine of total war. He suggested that never again would there be such a designation as "noncombatant." Yet, like Mitchell, he looked upon this prospect with a certain cheeriness, as one who kills only to be kind. "Mercifully," he wrote, "the decision will be quick in this kind of war, since the decisive blows will be directed at civilians, the element of the countries at war least able to sustain them. These future wars may yet prove to be more humane than in the past in spite of all, because they may in the long run shed less blood."

In describing the horrors of a bombing attack over a heavily populated city, Douhet vastly underestimated the bomb load, speed and altitude of the plane but embellished the grisliness by fancying that bombers would spray poison gases over the ruins. He recalled a fatal panic that ensued at Brescia during World War I when, in the midst of a funeral ceremony, someone looked up and mistook a large bird for an airplane. Such ludicrous fright would be multiplied a thousandfold, so that the future war would end this way: "The time would soon come when, to put an end to horror and suffering, the people themselves, driven by the instinct of self-preservation, would rise up and demand the end of the war—this before their army and navy had time to mobilize at all!"

In this blitzkrieg what might happen on the ground or at sea would be irrelevant. Air power, capable of "breaking down the material and moral resistance" of the enemy, was the one essential precondition of victory.

I did not read Douhet when I was growing up in the thirties, but if I had I would certainly have dismissed him as the creator, or the victim, of a fantasy that was peculiarly fascistic. Those who were to be my commanders and those others who were to be my enemies seemed to have followed him more closely. I came to Douhet late and read him in the light of Guernica, Coventry, Dresden, Berlin, Schweinfurt and Hiroshima. That post-facto look gives his writing a glow of fulfilled prophecy despite some monumental errors.

Douhet had dismissed World War I dogfights as "aerial knight errantry" which would have to be supplanted by "a real cavalry of the air." Furthermore, he singled out the heavy bombers as the invincible heavy dragoon of that cavalry. "A slower, heavily armed plane, able to clear its way with its own armament, can always get the best of a faster pursuit plane," he wrote. "A unit of combat composed of slower heavily armed planes is in a position to stand up to the fire of enemy pursuit planes and carry out its mission successfully."

That theorem stood as holy writ in the minds of airpower believers until August 17, 1943, when we were to test it over Schweinfurt.

Douhet found a congenial environment for his fancy in Fascist Italy. Billy Mitchell had it harder. He challenged the American military establishment not by putsch but by shouting his rebellion to the rank and file and to the public. He brought his campaign to a climax after a series of ghastly military air crashes that shocked the nation. Called upon to comment, he issued a statement to the press calculated to explode the issue, his superiors and perhaps himself: "These actions are the result of the incompetency, the criminal negligence and the almost treasonable negligence of our national defense by the Navy and War Departments . . . our pilots know they are going to be killed if they stay in service . . . in the old flaming coffins that we are still flying. . . . As a patriotic American citizen, I can stand by no longer and see these disgusting performances . . ."

He had made his court-martial inevitable. General Pershing, that earthbound hero, unwittingly obliged Mitchell by acting the part of a dinosaur on the way to extinction. He referred to Mitchell's behavior as symptomatic of the "Bolshevik bug" that was loose and had to be exterminated. Rallying to Mitchell's side and testifying for him were the young airmen of World War I, regardless of politics: Fiorello La Guardia, then a congressman, not yet the mayor of New York, Ira Eaker, Carl (Tooey) Spaatz, Hap Arnold and his wife, Bea, both of whom had done much to plan Mitchell's defense which was more like a suicidal offensive.

Mitchell's supporters were young then—mere majors and colonels. By the time of Schweinfurt they had risen to be generals in command of the American Army Air Forces, not quite an independent arm but nearly so. They had wandered in the desert sharing the guilty verdict handed down by Billy Mitchell's court-martial. Mitchell had been suspended but chose to resign. In 1942 Mitchell had been long dead and enshrined though never pardoned.

Colonel Perera had followed the careers of Mitchell's disciples. He noted in a report that the Air Corps Tactical School at Maxwell Field "did not find favor with the higher echelons of the Army" and had been discontinued. Nevertheless, he added, "certain former students had found their way into the intelligence branch of the Office of Chief of Air Corps."

They were in fact the new Brass, and by December 1942 they had perfected the machinery that would send me and my crewmates to Schweinfurt. They themselves had not yet considered that distant German city on the Regnitz. Only Perera and his fellow target pickers seemed to be aware of it.

Certainly few of us who bombed it had heard of the city. We were total strangers. I still know little about the place though it lingers in my mind with greater persistence than do many cities that are far dearer to me.

3

At the time of Billy Mitchell's court-martial I was still playing with toy soldiers—cardboard figures, four or five inches tall, standing on little bases of wood. They whirled and fell with gallant grace before a rubber-band cannon. They were all infantry or cavalry. I did not actually conceive of a personal relationship with an airplane until several years after Lindbergh flew the Atlantic. Then, it was true, I came to worship at Lindbergh's shrine. I fancied myself in love with a girl who shared my devotion to Lindbergh and to the idea of flight. Since we lived with half the country between us, our passion was largely literary and could therefore accommodate the latest news of Lindbergh as if he were part of our love life.

Actually, my family was so rigidly antimachine that neither I nor any of my brothers or my sister ever sat behind the wheel of an automobile until World War II. We had an aunt who owned a car but never drove it.

When we were very young we dreamed of travel by camel or elephant, but a carburetor was an unattractive mystery. If one could fly by verbal legerdemain I would have done so.

I grew up confusing myself with a plumed knight and an airplane with a horse. I did not imagine that I needed to trouble myself with the mechanics of a plane any more than the average knight worried about the biology of his steed. While I was yet a boy we moved from the Appalachian isolation of Scottdale, Pennsylvania, with its shady streets, turn-of-the-century frame houses and uniformed bands tootling in the park. I carried with me my tricycle and the memory of a happy, pungent gunpowder scent that preceded each Fourth of July as my father accumulated the ritual ammunition. Also in the baggage of my mind was the sign of the fiery cross burning in the blue hills. The Ku Klux Klan in those years and in that corner of Pennsylvania was purely a racket, extorting tribute from businessmen and professionals. We, along with a handful of other Jews, Catholics and the very few blacks on the outskirts of town were happily exempt because we served as ritualistic enemies. Beyond being deprived of the right to pay dues I can recall no other serious disability that was put upon our family by the Klan. My father's store went bankrupt without any help from them.

We moved from there by train. Any train ride is memorable to a boy, but this one was particularly grand because I went to sleep in a Pullman berth as we whipped around the horseshoe curve near Altoona with its great coal fires blazing in the night. We settled in Brooklyn near Gravesend Bay on the Narrows, that strait between Staten Island and Long Island. On that pebbly beach the bodies of calves and goats, bellies all bloated a ghastly gray, washed up from passing freighters to delight a growing boy's taste for the awful. On Sunday mornings we would read the comics aloud on the pleasant lawns of Fort Hamilton, which I thought no more a military facility than Flatbush was a bush. The occasional black cannon covered with tall grass I took to be purely ornamental.

I pass over the frantic joys, awkward triumphs and abashed defeats—sexual, artistic, literary and social—of my adolescence because in general outline they can be found in most novels, even if inadequately treated, or in the memory of any man who has ever been a boy. There are distinguishing and possibly interesting particulars in my case, but they have no bearing on the battle of Schweinfurt.

In the early thirties as a high-school student I was given to a lofty aestheticism with emphasis on French literature. In the late thirties, as a neophyte journalist, I plunged into political radicalism. In 1941 I was working for an organization which aided Jewish refugees. My job—actually my only real duty though I bore the impressive title of Assistant to the Executive Chairman—was to decipher and summarize foreign cables that told of Jews struggling to extricate themselves from the tightening noose in Germany.

When not thus engaged I was condemned to leisure on the job and spent my time contemplating people who were conspicuously flaunting their usefulness. Among these was a very energetic and sparkling young woman in a flaring green skirt whom I ogled, followed and besieged until she consented to have lunch with me. I discovered later that she feared a sly management plot to subvert the union's organizing campaign and checked with the shop steward before we met.

In short order she stopped reporting to the union and we married. Two months and a week after our wedding the Japanese attacked Pearl Harbor, and a week after that I enlisted. I assumed I was only one jump ahead of my draft board.

The Air Corps was not accepting applications for aircrews from married men, and so I threw myself on the mercies of my classifications officer. He spotted on my employment record a job I had held as script reader in the story department of Paramount Pictures. This was a name that activated the computer of his mind, which flashed to film, thence to projectionist, and thus to the Signal Corps. I had no objection.

I found myself in the company of five or six others whose prewar careers led the minds of their respective classifications officers into the same deep rut as had my own. A truck deposited us in front of a highly nervous officer at a signal post in Fort Dix, New Jersey.

I was astonished to find my first commanding officer throwing a tantrum. "I'm trying to close out this fucking outfit," he yelled. "What the hell do I want with you!"

It was my first experience at feeling totally inanimate. Eventually the officer signed the appropriate bill of lading for me along with the other freight. We all stood there as if the matter did not concern us. Actually we were there as a result of a typographical error. A clerk had transposed a number or two. We had been meant to staff a signal company in the West Indies, we were told later, but that consignment had been shipped out by the time the error was discovered. Our bodies were thus deposited at the feet of the perplexed signal officer at Fort Dix.

In the months that followed I learned to make my bed

with boxed corners. I did not have to do it often, because I rarely slept in it. Most nights I hitchhiked to my wife in New York and came running back to make reveille in the company street before daybreak. The nights were fine, but the days were deadly dull. We tended the fires in the furnace room beneath the signal office. We cleaned gigantic malodorous vats in the kitchen. In desperation some of the recruits learned to climb telephone poles and became linesmen. This did not seem attractive to the rest of us.

The master sergeant, when not drunk, was a genial man who had been in the service so long he had come to think that the best way to run an outfit was to let it alone. One day he roused himself to the brutal truth that he had on his hands some dozen civilians in uniform who had never had a day of basic training, never shouldered a pack, never slithered under barbed wire, never been properly yelled at. He found this incredible but at once undertook the responsibility for our training.

He trotted us out to the field one afternoon close to the hour of retreat. He lined us up and exhibited in his two hands a rifle. He said, "This is a rifle," and flung it at me. I caught it and nodded in recognition. He told us how to open the breech, load it, cock it, fire it, shoulder it. We did not actually fire, because to use the range would have required the sergeant to make some explanations to somebody and that might have made trouble. When each of us had had a close look at the rifle, had fondled it and shouldered it, he took it away and told us, "That's it, you've had your basic training. Right? It's on the fucking record, see?"

We nodded agreeably, rather pleased in a way, since, bored as we were, we did not fancy basic training. We

33

thought in our innocence that if the Fort Dix Signal Company should ever decide to join the war we would catch on, somehow.

The sergeant then retired to his desk and we to our drudgery or our sacks. The war seemed immeasurably far away. I seemed irrelevant. The refugees wandering over the face of the earth whose affairs I had chronicled in my civilian days were in another world. Before I enlisted I had at least heard reports of battle. Now the dying were shut out. I was playing not war but soldier in a preposterous game that had no time limit. We were misplaced, forgotten, and we lost all hope that someone would find us, dust us off and use us for something.

Then came liberation. The Air Corps, hard pressed for usable bodies, had declared that it would accept married men and, what is more, would offer a $2,000 bonus to all volunteers who would qualify as flying personnel and who would survive to the end of the war.

There were four of us who came magnificently alive at the news. The army doctor added a few pounds to my weight, which was below the minimum. I went south to where aircrews were training in perpetually blue skies. Another doctor did not cavil at my weight but found an erratic muscle in one eye. It would present no problem, he thought, except when I would need it most. He could not recommend me for pilot school. Why not navigation school? Why not, indeed? I had not yet learned to drive a car; a plane could wait. The important thing was to fly. And navigation—what with sextants, astrocompasses and gorgeous maps—struck me as altogether fascinating.

They took me despite my lack of poundage, my unmilitary bearing and my undependable ocular muscle.

They did not know that my basic training had been useful chiefly as an anecdote or that the only time I had ever fired a weapon was in a shooting gallery. When I considered the dubious material I offered to a cadet school and the willingness with which that school accepted me I realized that the war must be going badly indeed.

I had tried to follow the war as best I could in the hermetic atmosphere of the barracks. The Germans were tearing through Libya, the Crimea and the Caucasus, while the Japanese had taken or were taking the Philippines, Singapore, the Aleutian Islands, New Guinea and Guadalcanal. They were rounding up Jews in Paris for "resettlement" in the camps of the East. And —as we later learned—the Reichsbank directors at a formal dinner were congratulating themselves at the phenomenal rise in stocks of gold plucked from the teeth or stripped from the fingers of resettled corpses.

I was confronting other problems—of shameful frivolity. I had gone through the most rigorous and classically academic of high schools that boasted a newspaper in Latin and a championship chess team. After that I found college a bit elementary. Now here was I at a military prep school, being braced by upperclassmen with my chin touching my chest and unspoken snobbish ironies whirling in my head. I moved, ate, digested and slept on command. I fussed on parade with white gloves and shining sword. I had played with cardboard soldiers so often in my childhood, but I had never been one. I found it mindless but funny. Yet, after I could stand at attention for hours in the Southern sun with my sweat running rivulets into my eyes, when I could run for miles and miles and discover that neither my heart nor my lungs would actually burst and would in time subside within their skeletonic cage, I found it not too painful.

All this, I told myself, is sanctified by tradition like the ringing of bells for the new year, like the lighting of fireworks for the Fourth of July, like the marriage vow. It may have little to do with the winning of wars or the torture of Hitler's victims, but it is no doubt venerable. And the marching tunes were catchy. The war would have to wait. The agonies of others would have to wait while we flourished our sabers and officers gigged me for letting the dust of my footlocker soil their white gloves.

We had time for such lessons in military courtesy as the leaving of calling cards on reporting to a new post. But the folderol did not distract too greatly from the study of navigation. Making a navigator out of me was easier, I think, than teaching me to be a military gentleman. I found it altogether delightful to use the same stars as had my illustrious Elizabethan or even Phoenician predecessors on their more leisurely excursions across the seas.

And then there came the airplane. It was a training plane—a two-seater. It tossed the sun back so that one had to squint at it. I remember it now, after so many years and so many flights, with a fidelity and a freshness one usually reserves for initiations into more carnal love affairs.

In airplanes nowadays I do not fly; I am flown. In that little training plane I flew. Never mind that I did not manipulate the controls; the wings of the plane were my wings. When we banked and side-slipped down the blue sky, and the earth stood its checkerboard fields on end to see us pass, I felt the wind we made and saw the world for the first time. If one could recall how the first breath of air tasted on the infant tongue, that might compare with one's first flight. It is a truism that war corrodes like gangrene; and it is also true and well chronicled that it grants moments of splendor, but on that first flight, war put on an air of unutterable innocence.

By the end of 1942 I had learned to dogleg around the Louisiana bayous and to follow all the clues the stars might leave.

My wife, who had given up her job with the Office of War Information, and I had been sharing a house in Monroe with another cadet couple. It was a shaded frame house of uncertain age and style, joined to our land-lady's. She was a cordial lady of Italian origin who had come down from the North. She reveled in the Southern tradition and swallowed it whole, scarcely pausing to distinguish between the digestible and undigestible portions. She treated us very well although it was plain that we were not Southern and not crisply Yankee either. She knew she had rented to Jews and Armenians and it is only fair to say that she would have done so with equal graciousness even if the war had not made such alien guests a patriotic burden.

Our relations remained cordial until she told us how her precocious twelve-year-old son chased a Negro woman off a bus because she took a seat beside his. After that we paid our rent but cut our landlady dead socially. We felt warmed by our virtue. It was part of our innocence. When my Armenian friend, the son of a Christian minister but blessed with an aquiline nose of majestic proportions, took the brunt of the fussy, scarce-ly articulated anti-Semitism endemic in the camp or town, we thought the joke was on the anti-Semites because they had missed their target. We had not yet heard of Auschwitz and very likely we would not have believed the truth if we were told it. We talked of fascism, freedom and class war, and it seems now that we did so as little boys caricature reality by scrawling a stylized anatomy on a wall.

In this setting of easygoing anticipation Esther tightened the drama to a new pitch. Were we in bed or window shopping along De Siard Street or strolling along the river? I do not know. Vaguely I hear as background to my recollection a cracked and wheezy recording of an aria from *Orpheus and Eurydice* which our Armenian friends habitually played. So I suppose we were in our room with the street lamps and the pecan trees making shadows on the bed.

It was doubtless there that Esther suggested that she would like to have a child.

"You know, of course, I might not . . ." I began.

She nodded. "I know. Then at least I'd have a child."

I looked at her in wonder.

In January 1943 I found myself a second lieutenant with silver wings. I bought myself a handsome belted trench coat and a pair of pinks. I was presented a set of calling cards, inscribed with my name and rank in a flowing, pseudo-Spencerian type face. I was ready for war.

I was sent to Salt Lake City, where flying personnel were being sorted out and dispatched by the luck of the draw to wherever a body with certain specifications was needed to fill a manning table. I was not in Salt Lake long. I remember only the astonishment of walking down an ordinary street and beholding a snow peak at the end of it, incongruous as a vision of a tiger at a kitchen sink. The blinking neon of diners and gas stations, suggestive of humankind, seemed like fungi sprouting from the crevices of awesome wonders.

The chancy workings of army assignments packed me off to Sioux City, Iowa, to fill the last vacancy in the last crew of the last squadron of the newly formed 379th Bombardment Group. When the orders came down I had no reason to cheer or to groan. I knew nothing of the group except that it flew B-17s.

There are those who ask how one may speak affectionately of a collection of metal plates, bolts, nuts, wires, plexiglass, turbines, motors, assorted sensory equipment and various expressive needles and gauges.

Bohn Fawkes, the co-pilot of my new crew, told me how he came to entertain what he called "comradely feelings" toward machines. He was wonderfully attuned to the hums, whirs, quirks and moods of an aircraft. I was to learn how he could wheedle a plane into flying even when it was torn by shells and when its motors were gasping with a moribund splutter. I have known friends and even lovers less sensitive to the vagaries of each other than were Bohn and a B-17.

He had worked his way through engineering school by hauling house trailers on weekends. A trip from his native Minneapolis to Saginaw or Kalamazoo or Chicago might net him thirty-five dollars free and clear. That plus the hundred dollars a year he earned from ROTC got him by. The loads he towed were some twenty-five feet long. They had no brakes and, like an elephant in hot pursuit, tended to climb up the rear end of the tow car unless kept in place by gentle handling. The cars they gave Bohn were old and usually eccentric. One had to get to know them quickly.

Once, he told me, he had to haul a trailer up through North Dakota to within two miles of the Canadian border in a winter's cold that ate through leather and bit into bone. He babied his tow car with its burned-out bearings and stayed awake for seventy-two hours cajoling masses of beaten and weary machinery through the snows of arctic Dakota and Minnesota.

Though I had no such intimate experience with machinery, I had no contempt for it. To me an airplane was not so much a machine as a carapace inhabited by animate creatures such as I was used to loving. To me, hard metallic things come alive only when they are haunted. Thomas Wolfe, giving his heart to ships, thought them "alive with the supreme ecstasy of the modern world." I did not think of that line when first I saw a B-17 fly, but I marveled at the sweep of the wing and the great tail soaring more like the fin of a sea creature than any part of a bird, and the plexiglass nose—of the sort that was to be my particular home— riding the wind like a bubble.

That nose had a characteristic smell of hot metal in an airless space which I learned to endure. Later I would associate it with the pungent spice of gunpowder and with the numbing cold of five miles up.

We who lived in the nose watched the world slip beneath us in aspects as variable as the sea, now gentle, now menacing, never flat and neatly framed as by a train window. We saw the world round and rolling, barely tolerating on its surface the human ephemera of cities.

The furniture of the nose was simple: for me, a shelflike desk, a .50-caliber machine gun, a magnetic compass, a panel of instruments that would give me useful information such as the altitude and the airspeed. All this was on the port side. Under the starboard window was my drift meter, used to gauge the wind from a corner of a forest, a bend in a river, a whitecap on an empty ocean, or anything that might be isolated and observed as it slipped beneath two cross hairs. Above me was a dome through which I might determine the relationship of the stars to earth and so deduce our position.

At the tip of the nose was the bombardier's perch. There was the mounting for the celebrated Norden bombsight, a panel of data-yielding dials and an array of switches that would enable the bombardier to correct the plane's heading, open the bomb-bay doors and finally release the bombs from their racks. Projecting from the plexiglass tip of the nose, like an insect's sting, was a .50-caliber that could be swung in an arc far more ample and meaningful than that of the navigator's gun.

Up a hatchway at the navigator's back was the cockpit where pilot and co-pilot rode as on the bridge of a ship. They saw the sky and the curve of the far horizon but not the swell of the sea or the rich details of the earth. Behind them would stand the engineer, peering over the pilot's shoulder at gauges that monitored the health and functioning of four engines. Above him was the top turret of twin .50-caliber guns that could spin around the sky, their arc cut out only enough to keep the engineer from blasting the plane's tail.

Beyond the engineer's station was the bomb bay. The bombs would be stacked in racks on either side where the armorers would have hung them up like huge black fish fixed on skewers. Between the rows of bombs ran a shiny steel catwalk. Walk that narrow trestle with the bomb bay closed and you are in a creature's dark belly. But when the doors are open beneath your feet you clutch the cables on either side to steady yourself against the winds and against the terrible nothingness that spreads between you and the indifferent distant earth.

Step beyond the door at the far end of the catwalk and you are in the radio operator's room, where he can monitor a friendly beam or send an SOS. Ordinary bombing crews do not clutter up the airwaves with less urgent messages. The roof is of plexiglass that can be pulled back to allow a .50-caliber gun to be mounted in its place.

Aft of the radio room the waist begins to taper. At altitude its rounded metal walls can freeze the flesh that touches it. Plexiglass port windows line each side, but these are opened in combat to let the guns command the largest possible strip of sky.

At the touch of a lever and with a motor's whine the ball turret descends behind the radio room to receive into its womb the curled form of the belly gunner.

At the end of the funnellike fuselage, behind the soaring finlike tail, are the twin guns that cover the plane against attack from the rear. There is enough space for a man to sit or crouch on his knees, to wield his two .50-calibers, to change his belts of ammo, but that is the limit to his maneuverability. There are windows on each side of his head and one in front of him as he faces backward toward the threat from six o-clock.

Those tail guns marked a major advance over earlier B-17s which had not been kindly received at their combat debut. A prototypical B-17 had been designed in the midthirties to celebrate an anniversary of the Air Corps. It had been used on a flight around Latin America confusedly billed as a "goodwill mission." Although a flight of bombers does not seem to be the happiest symbol of international harmony, the only hostility to the plane came from Army and Navy Brass who wanted it clearly understood that the Flying Fortress was never to be used except to facilitate operations of the senior services.

The plane went through a series of transformations, its tail rising more imposingly with each step up the alphabet of its evolution. In 1941 the B-17E was introduced to the RAF when they were attempting daylight missions. The results were disastrous. The planes were either shot down or so shot up that they could not fly again. The British called the B-17E the "Flying Target" and decided that henceforth they would fly by night. The Germans called it the "Flying Coffin." It was then that the twin-fifties were mounted in the tail and the B-17F was born.

It had a wingspan of 104 feet and it weighed some 34,000 pounds. It flew at over a hundred and fifty miles an hour. Such data are as meaningless as the chemical analysis of a human being. When we came to know our B-17F, *Tondelayo,* we gave ourselves to her completely, mingling our lives with her machinery, but that happy state, like most marriages, took time to achieve. When, in Oklahoma City, she was given to us and we to her, it would have been hard for me to believe that a part of me would one day follow her down through green viscous waters to founder in sand and sludge at the bottom of the sea where now she rests.

I think that Johnny, our pilot, gave himself to *Tondelayo,* but I am not sure. Johnny communicated with me exclusively through banter. I do not think I ever had a sober, serious word with him. He wore his hat crushed and cocky. A toothpick dangled from his lips. He was "raunchy," a then fashionable adjective used to conjure up the image of a casual, sloppy, spitting, cussing hero. The war was laid out for Johnny like a

43

scenario. His postwar visions included a "great big yellow cock-wagon" in which he would orgiastically careen through the streets of his native town in Nevada. It is as a cliché that I remember Johnny, and that's a pity because he used that cliché only as something in which to wrap himself against the wind and his crew-mates.

I never saw him drunk. He drank only because his image drank. He was a slave to that image as he might have been a slave to his car, forever polishing it and stepping back to view it from this angle or that. It was hard for me, or, I believe, for anyone else, to see behind that image.

Johnny salted his language in the ritual way, but what was said between the expletives was so innocuous that it could go down in a kindergarten. The trouble was that Johnny was in fact unreal, a phantom pilot waiting for the movie to unwind to the big parade scene with the high-school band tootling and him ready to walk bare-foot over acres of tits. This was the stuff of GI poetry. The same vision hovered in many mirrors when flyers put on their grins before storming a stateside town on an overnight pass.

We did not know that Johnny lived only in that final scene. Certainly we in the nose were unaware of the secrets of the cockpit, although these could have meant our deaths. We did not know of the personal drama unfolding at the controls. Actually neither Bohn nor Johnny nor our very discreet engineer, Larry, realized at the time just what was happening.

It was decades later—after *Tondelayo* lay at the ocean bottom, after all of us had learned to live somehow without the war and after some of us had domesticated the memories of battle into quite useful household ghosts—that Bohn told me of his first intimations of Johnny's response to crises.

There was a flight out of Wendover, Utah, for example. Wendover Field is a bowl rimmed by rocks, and in wintertime it is covered by a lid of leaden cloud. To leave it one had to close-spiral up through the muck to where the sun shone over a limitless pad of white tufted wool. On a December day Johnny took a B-17 off and up to clear the rocks and head for El Paso. An instructor pilot assigned to check Johnny out was curled up in the nose, sleeping off a hangover. Bohn, in the co-pilot's seat, was fiddling with an oxygen mask with which he was totally unfamiliar.

All around them was an opaque gray cushion, obliterating the horizon and all reference points by which one normally judges one's place in the world. In such circumstances a flyer assumes that the ceiling is up and the floor is down. It is the merest shadow of a certainty, but one clings to it.

Bohn was trying to mold the rubber mask to the outlines of his face, wondering about the fit below the cheekbones, when he felt a tap on his knee. He turned to see Johnny gesturing toward the co-pilot's wheel, the signal for Bohn to take over. Bohn found the wheel limp. This is a realization of that most terrifying dream of total impotence in which one screams and finds that the scream is silent.

Bohn glanced quickly at the instrument panel. The plane was climbing at a rate of 1,500 feet per minute; the airspeed was dropping. The needle and ball which indicate the plane's posture had collapsed. At that moment the cloud over Wendover parted slightly and Bohn caught a glimpse of the ground, but, unbelievably, it was over his shoulder out the top hatch where only sky should be. The plane had stalled, had flipped on its back and was about to enter a spin which would surely tear the wings off and send it plummeting like a rock to earth. In fact Bohn had only seconds to set the world aright, restore the sky to its place above and the earth below.

He eased the plane around to where he could nose it down. He put it into a dive and felt the wheel's resistance stiffen. He had to pull out of the dive with a force of two or three g's, he later estimated.

Just before the pullout the instructor had been jolted out of his private fog. He was clambering into the cockpit when the pullout sent him reeling back into the nose. When Bohn had managed to fly level once more the instructor picked himself up from the floor, climbed into the cockpit and asked in a towering military rage who the fuck was flying the fucking wings off the fucking plane. Bohn, hearing no confession from Johnny, kept silent. The instructor, noting Bohn at the controls, saw no reason to think he had not been flying all along.

In discussing the matter years later Bohn had a simple explanation for his behavior: If Johnny would not turn himself in, that was his problem; Bohn was not going to do it for him.

Bohn took whatever black marks the instructor felt impelled to file in his report. For punishment he was ordered to fly on instruments all the way to El Paso. It was all right with him, he commented later. He needed the practice anyway. Johnny never said a word.

No one said a word for the next thirty-five years. That's what it means to cover the weakness of one man with the honor of others. It preserves the weakness along with the honor. Johnny's lapse was a small thing in itself—though it might have meant ten dead men shattered like china plates on the ground. It was merely the momentary vagary of a half-trained pilot. Nobody read the omen which, as seen in retrospect, clearly foretold disaster.

Bob, our bombardier, who shared the nose with me, was so robust a character he made the rest of us seem fragile. He bounced and laughed so heartily it took me weeks and months to understand that he had an aspect that was not bubbles and sunshine. It was decades before I learned of Bob's agony. Thirty-five years later he still wakes in rage and terror that he cannot define. When I talk about the war he marvels, but finds in his mind no flash of recognition. "Was I there?" he asks. "Did it happen?"

He is in a wheelchair. He was stricken with polio right after the war. "Not service-connected" was the VA verdict, and he was fobbed off with a minuscule pension. The bombing trade he had learned in the war was of no use to a man in peacetime with a growing family to feed.

Bob had come out of a Minnesota farm where joyless poverty was somehow equated with virtue. He tried to manage an adolescence on the fifteen cents his father paid him for every rat he caught in the barn and threw to the army of ravening cats. War emancipated him from familial servitude, offering him a defense job at eighty-five dollars a week with time off for poker if he kept out of sight.

The war was a great new game. He enlisted to gain his choice of jobs in the service. He tried pilot training but washed out and became our irrepressible bombardier.

In his postwar life as in his battle days he met every crisis with fierce action, utterly uncalculated but often precisely right. Broke and forever bound to his chair, he scrounged among his belongings for something to turn

47

into money. He found an old cement mixer and put it out
on his lawn with a "To Rent" sign on it. One man rented
it, and others followed. He bought another mixer, then
some lawn mowers and a pickup truck. And so the rental
business grew. He and his wife plugged away at the
enterprise, raised seven children and then separated.
Now he wins archery awards, plays basketball and
claims that he can square-dance in his wheelchair. With
savage certainty he proclaims a path to salvation by
diet, vitamins and proper bowel functioning. Bob has
kept his rage for all these years, using different masks
and different targets.

Our tail gunner was a saw-toothed, swarthy little
man, a street-wise Ulysses, cunning and winning. Mike
could have been a trader in a Moroccan bazaar or a taxi
driver with a detailed guide to the whims of every
passenger's flickering heart and mind. He was a superb
gunner, but if he had not been he would have made me
think he was.

Our radioman had style. I have seen Duke, wearing
his fatigues, with a mess kit hanging from his belt, lean
forward and toss a salute. In the process he would so
patronize a hapless officer that the latter would slink
away to hide his brass. I have heard other men say that
when they salute an officer it is their way of sending the
message "Fuck you." Duke delivered that message with
punctilio. Of course, within the crew we were never on
saluting terms except under formal compulsion. (Actually I can't remember any such circumstance, but I must
assume that there were occasions demanding such
"chicken-shit." We were more or less in the Army.) Duke
was tall and smooth. He had a mustache like a pencil
line and a flashing style. He was the soul of urbanity,
but he suffered yokels gladly.

There were three others in that crew, but I am embarrassed to confess that now their faces are blurred. Perhaps this is because their subsequent vanishing was so spectacular that I can now recall only their absence and not their presence.

I came into the crew as a last-minute replacement. My predecessor had been competent, I am told, but worried because he was operating under what he conceived to be double jeopardy. If he had to parachute into enemy territory and was captured, he thought, he would be singled out for particularly nasty treatment not only as a member of a crew that had dropped bombs but also as a Jew. (Insistent that every soldier have the comfort of the particular last rites enjoined by his upbringing, the Army had stamped every dogtag with an initial indicating the soldier's presumed faith. And every American soldier was expected to have one of the standard religious affiliations. I suppose that if one wanted to fight the battle for agnostics and atheists one could have demanded an "A," but few Jews would try to dodge the "H" lest it be thought they were running to cover.)

I do not know why I never shared this nightmare of my predecessor. Perhaps it was because it seemed a bit obsessive to fasten on one conceivable disaster when the future had such an abundance of alarming possibilities. It was a refinement of terror which escaped my less sensitive antennae. In any case, one of the squadron navigators was assigned to serve as group navigator and my predecessor delightedly moved up to take his place with an older and more seasoned crew. In the irony that frequently accompanies such gambling my predecessor went down over Schweinfurt. For me as for all flyers such luck, however welcome, adds a drop of guilt to the cup.

I had fallen into this crew, but in a kind of puppy-dog innocence I behaved as if I had chosen and been chosen. I liked them. As for the upper Brass I was only dimly aware of them. I do not think that they were even dimly aware of me. Colonel Mo Preston made his way through lieutenants and lesser ranks like a rhino through high grass. In his wake fluttered the symbiotic birds that live on ticks of the royal beast: Mo's hand-picked majors—the genial, paunchy Shockley, the supercilious Culpepper, the cocky little Rip Rohr.

Do I remember accurately or did I look upon these masters of my fate with the mean spite of an envious underling? Mo Preston is now a general (retired). I am an ex-lieutenant. We sit in the kitchen of his Washington home and, over coffee and whiskey, trade stories of battles and high jinks. (It would be presumptuous to say that we fought or played together even though at times we were in the same square mile of shell-raked sky, for I knew him by rank and he knew me by number.)

We compare notes and, surprisingly, in some respects they tally. Major Shockley, General Mo confesses, proved a disappointment in combat. He had flown tow planes for RCAF gunners and was a competent flyer, but Mo observed that he tended to cover his eyes with his hands at the sight of enemy aircraft coming in his direction. It was an understandable and uncontrollable weakness in an otherwise good man, but General Mo thought it unpardonable in an operations officer. So he set him up as the man in charge of the officers' club. Shockley kept his rank and tried to earn it by running the best-stocked bar in the European Theater of Operations despite all the privations of war and the obstructionist tactics of military bureaucracy. The club was christened Duffy's Tavern after a radio show, and Shockley was celebrated

as Major Duffy. He had found his calling. General Mo
and I agree that if all of the officer corps had been
similarly slotted according to their abilities we might
have won the war sooner or with lighter losses or with
better grace.

Culpepper I recall as the "Milk-Run Major." General
Mo nods in agreement. "I transferred him out as soon as
I saw what was happening," he says. Not as fast as we
saw it, as I recall.

We both saw Rip Rohr as incredibly eager. The
General is more critical of his flying than I am, for, as a
navigator, I think it quite enough for a pilot to take off
and land with a modicum of safety, fly headings given by
the navigator, get out of the way of flak and flying
bullets and be prepared to ditch or crash-land without
tearing the plane apart. The finer points of a pilot's craft
elude my undiscriminating eye.

The memories of Carlson, though, are touchier. Swede
Carlson was my squadron CO. He was not a forbidding
type even to a lieutenant fresh out of navigation school.
The worst that could be said of him was that he had a
sense of humor that might have been acceptable at
a summer camp for not particularly gifted boys. With a
few drinks he thought it the soul of wit and good
fellowship to call the officers in his command to attention and then proceed to snip off their ties with scissors.
Harmless but boring.

The tendency to drink and snip ties was very likely a
product of the dust and tedium of Wendover that af-
flicted the squadron before I joined it. The field was
perpetually socked in. The town was unexciting. Sand
and salt blew in swirls or seeped invisibly through walls.
Salt and sand granulated the eyelids and put a furry
coating on the tongue. To be choked and imprisoned by

fog was obviously trying to Carlson's spirits. He drank too much, though nobody remembers any outrage committed by him that was insufferable by army standards. He was a friend of Mo's. Mo acknowledges as much. He found it a point of flinty honor, therefore, to break Carlson down from major to second lieutenant.

Perhaps, say my informants—for I was not there— Carlson finally went too far and cut the colonel's tie. In any case Mo retained Swede as squadron commander though he knew it would be hard for him to keep the respect of men who outranked him. Still, Carlson made it, says General Mo, in tones of pride, for a general, like God, shares the glory of those who triumph over the adversities he has put in their path. The legend has it that Swede agreed to accept the loss of rank and pay without a fight, but vowed that he would not go into combat until his rank was restored. And so it was, though Mo does not now remember such a vow.

The General, tall, a little stooped, is still imposing. I do not still clothe him in glory of the kind he wore when he was a young colonel and I was a younger lieutenant. He is touchingly proud of the 379th Bombardment Group and trots out the charts and records which show our outfit to have had the best score of bombs delivered and missions flown when weighed against losses of aircraft. It is gratifying to realize that one played—if that is the right word—on the winning team.

When rival generals recall that the 379th also held the highest VD rate in the ETO, Mo concedes only that we were virile to a fault. His gaffer's pride is unassailable. He would be proud of me too, if he could remember who I was. He would be proud of *Tondelayo,* but he cannot quite place her. He cannot even recall her spectacular end. But there were so many lovely machines that fell apart in flames or in water; I cannot fault this soldier who sits with me at the table mulling over old death-defying glories and laughing idiocies that are the stuff of reunions. They go down better with a bottle. They do not stand the sober light of noon too well unless one reminds oneself, as I do, that this crusty old general was not merely a lord of supper clubs, that he did not fling away young lives as if they were chips on a gambling table, that he too flew combat like the rest of us.

"Mo, when we went to Schweinfurt, did you reckon the cost? Did you think it was going to be worth it all?"

"How did I know? I was a plowboy like you."

4

In Sioux City before the war began for us I did not reckon Colonel Mo as one of us. And in any case I did not think of myself as dragging a plow through a rut. I was like a matador who never faced a bull. I delighted in the spangled suit and the music of a visceral minor key. Blood and death were leitmotifs in a very classy production number to which I was being allowed to contribute in a bit part.

Esther had come out to be with me on the last of my stateside stations. We were rounding out our honeymoon that had been a passionate, funny, loving and frustrating sequence of hellos and goodbyes on airfields throughout the Northeast, the South and the Midwest. We found a house on the edge of Sioux City. Our windows looked out on the grimmest of badlands—a somber moor with here and there a boulder casting shadows the color of clotted blood to invite the brain to eerie fancies. I remember the panorama as perpetually blanketed by a dun-colored sky.

When we were together we enjoyed the drama of the place. When Esther was alone—and that was quite often, as it turned out—she loathed it. She closed the curtains to wall away the moor and looked only out the door, where other houses straggled along a road that curved in a show of suburban charm.

I went on enjoying my window on the world. Our training was less than rigorous. Sioux City in the dead of winter offered no skies fit for an education in formation flying. So we flew south and west. We buzzed herds of cattle on the prairie and laughed to watch them scatter at the sound of our engines. Insulated by the metal of our plane and by our youth, rendered more mindless by the excitement of war and flying, we felt our power in the animal panic below. We could not hear the sounds they made in their terror.

We arranged convenient engine breakdowns where a crewman might know a girl or where there were towns with a reputation for dazzling corruption to which we aspired and which most of us never attained.

I returned one day to Sioux City to find we had moved to the center of town, safely away from the moors. I opened my arms to Esther and, in what I imagined to be a gesture of careless rapture, dropped my musette bag. Unfortunately, it contained a bottle of Canadian Club which shattered, stinking up the place and taking the edge off my homecoming.

It was then or shortly afterward that we learned we were going to have a child. And soon after that, with exquisite timing, the 379th received its orders to proceed to war. The conjunction of these events illustrates war's theatrical manner of confusing life and death.

Esther and I lost ourselves in a blur of tenderness in which the possibilities of danger for either of us registered in our minds like the barest shadow of a cloud puff over a landscape of prairie and hills.

We had the customary final leave and took it in New York, but thought to hedge the city away from us. We told the cabdriver to take us to the St. George. The hotel's name had stuck in my mind. I think I had it confused with a hotel in Brooklyn or perhaps in Oklahoma and had misplaced it in Manhattan. The driver bent upon us a compassionate and condescending gaze he kept for benighted foreigners. We noted it but paid it no mind. He drove us by ways that were strange to a dismal building in the East Twenties, a grimy structure with yellowed curtains flapping in the windows. God knows what color they were when they were new if indeed they ever were new. It was a fly-specked fleabag. Possibly in better days it might have been a whorehouse. We looked at it from the cab window and Esther rejected it with a violent shake of the head. "That's not it," I said. "I know," said the cabbie, and he drove us crosstown to the Brevoort.

What was to have been three weeks turned out to be four days. Carlson telegraphed me: "REPORT TO STATION ON OR BEFORE MIDNIGHT, APRIL FOUR, NINETEEN HUNDRED FORTY-THREE END." I pondered the Postal Telegraph form and wondered why the Army should have taken the trouble to spell out the year as if otherwise I might turn up on or before midnight in 1944 or 1945. I was impressed with the enormous resources of an army that could be so profligate with telegraphic wordage. Esther and I said goodbye again. It was only the separation, not the war, that troubled us. Neither of us, I believe, had any dire forebodings.

We went from Sioux City to Oklahoma to pick up our plane. Johnny, pulling his rank, had unilaterally decided its name. It would be *Tondelayo,* a character portrayed by Hedy Lamarr in *White Cargo,* a movie of explicit typhoons and implicit sex. Some GI cartoonists served their country well by painting the lady in a bra and a modest blur of a skirt, with her long pink legs dangling just outside the navigator's side window, where my .50-caliber would swing and where my name was lettered as it might be on an office door. It read "BENNY." I had never liked the name, but it was an abbreviation that came naturally to my crewmates. "I will know that it means me," I thought. "And that's enough."

Tondelayo had the smell of a new machine. I tried out my desk—a shelf that ran below the gun. I put my head into the astrodome. I peered at the cross hairs of my drift meter. I sat and stood and walked about the nose like a boy given a room to himself. So did we all. This was ours. It was a home of our own, a car of our own, a ship of our own. Her engines quickly took on a special sound unlike all other engines. We stood back and looked at her as horsemen look at the lines of a thoroughbred. We liked the way she lifted her tail. We admired her gleaming flanks. We watched her from the ground on her test flights. We followed her as she took off, climbed and wheeled, flinging back the sun. One B-17 is not like another. Each has its crotchets and its graces. Once it has absorbed its share of lives and deaths it can live, be loved and die.

Because we were issued fleece-lined flying caps and boots we thought it almost certain that we would wind up in Africa or the South Pacific. But the Army's logic cannot be depended on to be perverse. We headed across New England in formation. It was a cool and pleasant

58

April. Then suddenly it was a hard, wet winter again at Gander in Newfoundland. The weather was as unyielding as the brown-black rock and the leaden sky. Spring made itself felt only in the mud that lapped at the doors of the Nissen huts. Gulls screamed into the wind or perched on flat rocks washed black by the waves.

Inside the canteen, girls bulging beneath their mannish blue uniforms poured gallons of black tea. I caught cold and snuffled over the fumes of the kerosene stove in the barracks, furious at the indignity of such a piddling ailment at a time of crisis. A week went by with us perched like forlorn and stranded seabirds under angry clouds. There was a beauty in the place, but you had to have the cold wind taking you by surprise and snatching at your breath if you were to obtain the proper mood for it. Once that astonishment was tempered by repetition, the place grew deadly. One had to read the springtime changes in minutiae of mosses and lichen.

I do not recall my squadron or the larger world of the group during that week of waiting. I remember only my crew, possibly because we were thrown back on our own resources. More and more the crew and the plane were becoming the elemental unit, the nuclear family. It was around *Tondelayo* that we spun our loyalties.

In those days, before fear set in, there was only excitement and impatience. Bohn carefully tightened the lid of his reserve. Johnny nervously picked his teeth, slouched and grumbled. I wonder whether if it were not for that humiliating and dispiriting cold I might have noticed the interplay between Bohn and Johnny and the secret that was growing between them.

We had the sensation of being cut adrift. We aircrews were alone. The ground crews, armorers, MPs, intelligence officers, medics, clerks, cooks, drivers, experts on

59

poison-gas alerts and public relations, quartermasters, bartenders and all such paddlefeet necessary to keep crews aloft had gone by ship and would meet us in England.

England to me was a land of Victorian neo-Gothic castles, full of gingerbread and gimcracks, or else authentic battlemented ruins brooding over Welsh valleys or sitting on Cornwall's rocks. England was a landscape laced by railroad lines with stations built like cuckoo clocks bearing names such as "Asses-Milk-cum-Worter." The kingdom was inhabited by amiable bumblers with waistcoated paunches, by droopy knights on droopy horses, by admirals in tricornered hats and by metal-cuirassed dragoons brushing aside great crowds of tight-trousered dandies dripping elegant epigrams. And blooming orange girls would thrust their bosoms over their corset stays in Hogarthian theaters. My head was full of that literary-historical-mythological view of England which is absurd but highly accurate if somewhat incomplete, as I later discovered.

I was serious about the war only in my outermost cerebral shell. I could expound the political necessity for it. I thought I knew the meaning of Hitler in political and socioeconomic terms. I thought I knew what he meant in blood and torment, in the anguish of people I acknowledged to be vaguely my kin and in the anguish of others whose principles I shared. I had given the war my intellectual approval—vital to my participation, I like to think—but in my young provincial way I could not then imagine the quality of desperation that is beyond politics and which for millions was the actual meaning of Hitler and the war.

I dashed off a telegram to Esther calculated to inform

her of my destination while foiling the censors and/or the enemy: "ON MERRIE WAY," the cable said.

On April 30 a cold front moving north and east passed over Gander, bringing black squalls on its high chill wind. Toward afternoon the sky brightened. We were briefed by weathermen. We would follow in the wake of that front, climb over it and head to Ireland and thence to Scotland. We drew our charts and reckoned our headings based on the estimates of winds that were given us. We set our watches in a count-down ceremony—"Three, two, one, hack." We were attuned within half a second to the timetable of celestial bodies and to the standards of Greenwich, England.

Each crew would fly on its own. Our tight family of total strangers now would be drawn even more into itself. It was to be bounded within the frame and skin and plexiglass of *Tondelayo*.

In the late afternoon we loaded our gear into the nose, which soon filled with shapeless masses of gray-green duffle. I surveyed my tools: dividers, plotters, pencils. (Suppose one were caught at sea without a pencil! Lost forever! Phoenicians on a raft might have had time to fashion one out of flotsam and the keenness of their pre-technological minds. But at our airspeed a plane would run out of gas over the Arctic or off the coast of Africa while one tried to fashion a pencil in the sterile spaces of sky.)

Then there is Bowditch, that classic of navigation designed for mariners, and the Ageton volumes of tables. Do I have the tables for the right latitudes? How awkward to know the positions of Aldebaran south but not north of Miami! I have checked my little library for the fourteenth time. I have seen to my sextant. Now the dust settles and the crew climb in to take their places.

At 0740 Johnny unleashes *Tondelayo* down the runway, and we soar over the gray whitecapped water. I have given him a heading based only on the weathermen's predictions. These will do for a start but no more than that. I see the lights of a plane that took off before us heading far to the north of the course I have plotted.

Bohn Fawkes is on the intercom pointing out the disparity, which is strange, he says, considering that we are all bound for the same place. "One of us is wrong," I say, and I note with satisfaction that nobody asks which. Bob looks back at me from his bombardier's perch on the parachute bag and grins appreciatively.

We are only minutes into this solo voyage when I notice that my plotter, divider and pencils are sliding about on desk and floor, eluding my grasp and disappearing from the tiny puddle of light shed by my lamp. I gather what I can and attempt to hold on to the gadgetry while *Tondelayo* points her nose heavenward. I ask Johnny and Bohn to pause in their climb long enough for me to read our drift on a whitecap, but we are overtaking the front and they are anxious to get above it. We climb steeply and I follow Johnny's vagaries on my compass, keeping track of how far off he goes and for how long so that I can gauge how far we might be straying. I scribble notes to myself in an effort to be systematic and watch them slide away from me to the floor. We climb until we break out into a radiant night. There is a slice of moon not strong enough to make the stars fade but bright enough to set a gentle glow atop the boiling clouds beneath us.

I turn off my desk lamp. Bob has wrapped himself in his fleece-lined jacket, pulled his collar over his ears, and is sound asleep, shapeless as the parachute bags that make his bed. I put my head into the astrodome and feel myself a part of this creature, *Tondelayo*. I am a figurehead on a ship skimming a ghostly sea.

When I take my hands out of my gloves to grip the metal handle inside the astrodome my fingers burn at the icy touch. I wake up Bob so that he can time me for a two-minute shot with the sextant. First I must find the question mark in the sky which is Leo. (Out of respect for tradition I have tried to see a lion in that constellation, but I cannot.) I spot Regulus in its accustomed place and hold the dancing star in my sights while keeping the mercurial bubble on the level. I note my reading and go on to Arcturus blazing like a yellow beacon at the tip of the arc that plunges downward from the Dipper's handle. And then to Aldebaran.

"Where are we?" asks Bob.

"We're doing fine," I say with a navigator's unfailing assurance. He goes back to sleep while I use my readings to construct a small triangle on a chart of the ocean, which, except for latitudes and longitudes, fits Lewis Carroll's description of the ideal map—a perfect and absolute blank. The center of that triangle, I imagine, is where we are—off course. I wake Bob up and we do the whole thing over again.

I draw a line between my fixes and project it toward the coast of Norway. I calculate the wind that should be blowing and devise a heading to counter it. "Am I waking anybody up?" I call into the intercom. Bohn's voice is cool, gentle and teasing. "Can't sleep very well, can you?" he says. I give him the new heading, to which he responds with "Roger, wilco" and suchlike terms of the game we play.

I calculate new times for reaching Ireland and Scotland and give them to Bohn. The news is greeted by garbled, static-laden cheers from Mike in the tail and from Duke in the radio room. Bob waves his thumb upward and rolls over.

Then total silence—for the steady sound of *Tondelayo*'s engines no more intrudes upon my quiet than do the tides in my bloodstream. The plane rocks slightly as if in an uncertain sea. We skim the top of the frontal system, and clouds scud by in the moonlight. Saint Elmo's fire plays about the tips of the propellers as if we blazed in our own Aurora. We climb a bit higher.

I have time for another three-star fix which makes too large a triangle and a third which is nice and tight. The heading corrections now are small. I am more certain of my winds. I look up from my desk and find that the sky is paling. The stars are too faint now for an accurate shot. The night has been short, for, flying east, we have met the sun halfway across the ocean.

"Where are we, Benny?" someone calls.

How shall I say where we are? I can read off the coordinates on the chart, and my companions will rightly say, "Fuck off, Benny, where are we?" Even if the ocean, which I assume lies below these clouds, were visible in this luminous dawn it would be a wilderness of water. I look at my watch. "We are four hours, forty minutes and thirteen seconds from the coast of Ireland," I announce. I am uncertain of the minutes and I have thrown the seconds in for effect. Navigators must exude self-confidence or abdicate.

I turn my desk lamp off and watch the sun come up. It is not garish but still theatrical. The clouds grow pink below us and then the dazzling sun leaps up ahead of us, sparking the frost on the windows into gemlike stabs of light. I stumble past the hatchway up to the cockpit. Bohn turns to smile. Johnny, who has just been awakened by the sun bursting in his face, looks like a grumpy school kid. Larry, our engineer, stands behind Bohn's shoulder grinning cheerfully. Duke has not yet picked up a radio beam from Shannon. "Soon," I promise and hurry down to recalculate. If my arithmetic is right—and accuracy in simple calculation is not a strong point of mine—Ireland should be dead ahead. How does everyone know I am not taking them to Africa? How droll to land my B-17 in Fez where the sand makes for a magical sunrise over white minarets! "I must have mistaken Regulus for Deneb, sir . . . an astronomical error, sir, sorry."

One cannot shoot the sun when it reverberates in the sky. Once it calms down to a manageable ball of light and lifts away from the horizon one can indeed converse with it and derive at least the latitude. That's all very well for a seaman on a voyage of months or even days. We who have only a few hours need a more informative sky. But there is no landmark above and none below in the shifting mountains of cloud.

I can only guess at where we are by knowing where we have been an hour ago and how fast we got to that point from where we were an hour and a half ago, assuming that the winds have not changed too much in the intervening minutes either in direction or in velocity. I ponder imponderables and extend our course line closer and closer to Ireland, which seems a very small spot in so large a world.

"We should be over Ireland in thirty-seven minutes," I say with such assurance that I am convinced. A little while after that Bohn tells me we have picked up the Shannon beam. And, following my pencil and my hack watch, I deduce the moment we should be over land. Bohn begins the letdown. Gray murk blots out the sun, and *Tondelayo* rocks in the fog. Then as we emerge from the clouds and scudding wisps we see it.

"My God, it's really green."

"Green's green, but that fuckin' green is too much."

We left the drear of Newfoundland some ten hours ago and here we are in forest greens and meadow greens and sea greens and spring greens and river greens, varied as if all the colors of the world were green. I look down through the plexiglass and revel in Ireland. The intercom jangles with whooping, laughing, congratulatory jabber. I sort out the maps on the floor with the toe of my flying boot and pluck from the mess my charts of Ireland and Scotland. I find my way across Ulster, noting Belfast and a bluish lake out the starboard window. We sail over the Irish Sea, where causeways and cliffs appear as the mist parts. Scotland is a rosier, purplish country. That is the way I remember it, or is it the colors of the map that I recall?

We leap from the plane as an RAF sergeant and an American captain drive up in a jeep. After them comes an army truck and we prepare to clamber aboard.

"Whoa," says Bob. "Who's going to guard the sight?"

The Norden bombsight has been entrusted to us as if it were the secret weapon of the war, a magical gizmo that promises total victory. Our crewmen have stood guard duty over it as if they were in the infantry.

The captain says blithely, "Just put it down there on the edge of the runway. It'll be all right." We turn to each other in wonder and we look across the field where other secret bombsights lie upon the grass like litter baskets in a public park.

This is war!

5

Some of the 379th landed in Ireland, some in England, and at least one crew disappeared forever on the night of the crossing. Those of us who found our way to Prestwick were carefully treasured. We knew little of our own importance. To us the assignment seemed quite simple: we were to drop bombs where it would most discommode the enemy, return if possible, repeat the exercise twenty-five times. To speculate on what might happen after that was like worrying about the price of beer in heaven.

To our superiors we were rare prizes. General Eaker, my commander's commander, had watched and waited for us—that is, for any B-17 fitted out with young, well-fed, at least semitrained bodies and semi-intelligent minds. To hear the General recall how he came to be in England waiting for us, one would think he had been invited to join this war and decided that the only decent thing to do was to accept. He was dining with his friend General Hap Arnold in Washington early in 1942, as he tells the story. Said General Arnold, "Ira, I'd like you to go over and understudy the British Bomber Command so that you can run our effort when I get you some planes and crews." Eaker said thank you kindly and came over.

The prospect had seemed so promising then. The apostles of Billy Mitchell were going to be given the chance to prove that bombers could win a war with only the barest assistance from antiquated admirals and paddlefeet. By the time *Tondelayo* reached Prestwick a year had passed and the promise had not been fulfilled.

Eaker had settled in near High Wycombe at the country house of "Bomber" Harris. Arthur Harris, as chief of the RAF's Bomber Command, was then earning his nickname. He was absolutely convinced that bombing alone would win the war, and he is absolutely convinced now three and a half decades later—that bombing did in fact win the war.

He and his wife and daughter accommodated an enormous number of guests in their rambling old house which was not only a residence but a center for the propagation of the gospel of area bombing. This was a policy of saturating an enemy city with high explosives in the manner of Douhet's nightmare vision. Never was there a jollier devotee of *Schrecklichkeit*. Harris would lure his guests (and he reckons that he wined and dined five thousand of them in his war years) into his den for slide shows on the efficacy of his kind of warfare. Winston Churchill would come down regularly for a dose of indoctrination. Against those whose stomachs proved too delicate to digest the plain facts of bombing civilians Harris fired a battery of arguments: However horrible an air raid might be, civilians suffered far more in a blockade or a siege, to which strategies no one seemed to take exception. In any case the bomber was Britain's only recourse. It was the only way to draw the German Air Force away from Russia. In effect the air war, as Harris saw it, was the "second front" then being demanded so vociferously.

Precision bombing, he argued, was a very neat but unrealizable solution given the state of the art. To attempt it, as the Americans were proposing, was certain to be inordinately expensive in lives and planes, a cost which the RAF simply could not afford. Increasing one's own military casualties in a problematic effort to spare some of the enemy's civilians seemed to Harris to be quixotic and touchingly American. When he heard of Major Perera's suggestion of Schweinfurt he thought the target experts "completely mad."

The town was too small and distant to be hit with any force and precision, he felt, and if "by a miracle" all the ball-bearing factories in Germany were wiped out "this would only have embarrassed, not stopped, the German war effort." Harris had a word for planners like Perera and those in the British Section of Economic Warfare. He called them "panacea-mongers." Harris never thought of Germany as a diseased patient whose organs had to be neatly excised with a minimum of pain and blood. To him Germany was an all-too-healthy enemy whom it was quite proper to approach with meat ax or blowtorch.

Harris had come up from an assignment in Iraq, where he had led an antiquated, undermanned, ill-equipped and ill-maintained air force against mud-wall villages. It was not the likeliest proving ground for the war over Europe. He had arrived in England in time for the Blitz and recalls in his memoirs the nights when he climbed to the roof of the Air Ministry to look at the dome of St. Paul's rising out of "an ocean of fire." He listened to the "swish of the incendiaries."

It was nothing compared to what he would later send over German cities but enough to convince him that if the Germans had come over night after night and if at least some of their forces had managed to reach their targets, London would have died in a flaming hurricane. The Blitz stirred in Harris an ambition for revenge, but, looking back, he says it was only a momentary emotion and quite understandable in the circumstances. In his memoirs he indignantly denies that his vision of London and Coventry afire motivated his strategy. Vengeance was a passing and private sentiment, a luxury to which a warrior is entitled so long as it does not become public policy.

Harris had brought with him from his adventures in Iraq an engaging fancier of fish and butterflies. R. H. M. S. Saundby, in his full regalia as Air Vice-Marshal, would prowl among the hedges of High Wycombe in an endless search for butterfly specimens. It was Saundby who helped select the RAF targets and their code names, which reflected the Vice-Marshal's avocations. For example, Trout was his name for the great thousand-plane raid over Cologne. And Whitebait was code for Berlin. Harris notes that the names of butterflies and moths— such as the broad-bordered bee-hawk—do not lend themselves to top-secret telegrams, although Saundby pushed his *Lepidoptera* wherever possible.

The claims made for the early RAF raids of 1940 and 1941 were wildly exaggerated to boost home-front morale. In some cases the planes dropped only well-written leaflets suggesting that the Germans defect en masse. The attempts at bombing in those early months of the war were scarcely more effective than the leaflet raids. At best they were a nuisance to the Germans. In the beginning the British had been embarrassed by mounting raids that had little more purpose in them than simple terror. However, after the Germans had poured fire on the civilian center of Rotterdam in May 1940 the British felt less constrained. The War Cabinet authorized a hundred-bomber raid on the Ruhr as a gesture of defiance.

It was indeed no more than a gesture, because the bombers could not come close to finding any meaningful industrial targets at night in the blacked-out valley. The French were outraged because they wanted the RAF to blast the German tank columns then invading France. The Cabinet felt, however, that the moment called for a dramatic riposte to Rotterdam and some evidence of British power, which then was in short supply. Afterward it was said that, if nothing else, the Ruhr excursion did benefit France by "inviting" the Luftwaffe to retaliate against London, thereby sparing some of the aerial punishment that would otherwise have been inflicted on the French.

In August 1940 the Germans did bomb London. Actually it was the fault of a German navigator who unwittingly strayed from the oil tanks down the Thames. Londoners had been expecting to be bombed. The doomsday prophecies of Douhet, combined with the German reputation for beastliness in World War I, reinforced by Nazi outrages, had led the British to expect airborne atrocities ever since the first hours of the war.

No one could imagine that the Germans would be shy about introducing total war to England. Their Stukas had dived on refugee columns in Poland. Those dive bombers were by their nature tactical, not strategic weapons, designed to assist the ground force in its mission and not to act as independent agents of destruction. That distinction was lost on the refugees, but it was important to devotees of an autonomous air arm.

The Germans had in fact concentrated on a tactical air force. They did not shrink from strategic bombing à la Douhet out of moral scruples but because they doubted its effectiveness.

The British, although they approved of area bombing despite their scruples, were not completely convinced, either. Churchill told Sir Charles Portal, "It is very disputable whether bombing by itself will be a decisive factor in the present war. On the contrary, effects, both physical and moral, are greatly exaggerated." Churchill was not objecting to terror raids because they killed civilians but because the RAF flyers, gallant as they were, could rarely come to within five miles of their target.

Actually Churchill was fully prepared to use whatever horrendous weapons were available in the defense of England. If the Germans had invaded after Dunkirk as expected, Churchill was quite prepared not only to live up to his rhetoric in house-by-house resistance but also to use what was then considered the ultimate atrocious weapon for which the Huns of World War I had been damned—poison gas. (Americans too were to carry mustard gas with them when they invaded Italy, on the chance that the Germans would be the first to wreak the horror and thus lay themselves open to retaliation.)

The strategic-bombing enthusiasts could wring one hope from Churchill. "A different picture would be presented," he said, "if the enemy's air force were so far reduced as to enable heavy, accurate daylight bombing to take place." Harris saw no way to do this, but "heavy, accurate daylight bombing of factories" was precisely the American Air Forces recipe for winning the war. However, to wait until the Luftwaffe was whittled down did not suit American hubris or interservice politics.

In February 1942, just as Harris took over his job, Bomber Command received a new directive designating as a primary target "the morale of the enemy civilian population and in particular of the industrial worker." When Eaker settled in at High Wycombe shortly afterward Harris told him, "We have to use saturation bombing. We kill lots of workmen, true, but may I remind you, when you destroy a fighter factory it takes the Germans six weeks to replace it. When I kill a workman it takes twenty-one years to replace him."

Eaker replied courteously, "I'm sure that under the circumstances that's all you can do."

Over tea and dinner and drinks and cards Harris tried to talk Eaker into bringing his slowly accumulating Eighth Air Force into line with RAF thinking. As Eaker recalls those evenings, Harris would wheedle him like this: "While you're just beginning over here, why not come along with us on some night operations?"

Eaker: "No, Arthur, no."

Harris: "You see, we don't have enough planes to hit the Ruhr properly. If you could let us have even one group it would help."

Eaker: "No, we couldn't do that. B-17 engines throw a long flame, you see. We have to modify it for night work, and if we're going to make any changes it will be to turn the B-17s into a better daylight bomber."

From time to time Churchill would add his weight and charm to Harris's cause, for he had begun to modify his opposition to area bombing. "Just while your crews are training," the Prime Minister would say, "wouldn't it be valuable to them to go out on a few with Harris?"

And Eaker would answer, "No, sir, it wouldn't be valuable for what we want them to do. And night raids would give them a false sense of security."

It is best perhaps to leave the principal figures of that debate arguing in the spring of 1942 over a question that has long since been decided. As Harris now points out, the Americans who sought to evade the moral implications of the bombardment of cities by insisting on daylight precision ended the war at Hiroshima, thus accepting the terror principle in its ultimate expression with all its moral consequences. A wise and gentle Japanese in Hiroshima has found it fortunate that Japan did not have the atomic bomb. "We might have used it on the Americans," he said, "and then we would now have the problem the Americans have."

The war of 1940 to 1943 was not the war of 1945. In those early days, when *Tondelayo* had just come to Prestwick, there were still vestiges of an antique chivalry. Both British and German airmen, for example, made it a point to bring their bombs home—at risk to themselves and their home base—rather than drop them on some hapless enemy village when the prime target was covered by cloud.

Captured airmen were still being treated fraternally by their opposite numbers. Occasionally there would be salutes from flyers as they zoomed by each other in murderous passes. True, it was not quite as gallant as the behavior of a century earlier, when officers of opposing sides would ceremonially invite each other to be the first to fire. (History does not record the views of humbler victims of the ensuing slaughter.) That aristocratic age had given way to a far more murderous style

74

of destruction, though men still clung to the plumes and politesse of an earlier time. By the war's end, however, the lynching of airmen captured in German towns would be a commonplace.

Those who, like the eminent military historian Captain B. H. Liddell Hart, were appalled at the "terrorization policy of the RAF and the AAF" must now be beyond dismay and rage at the prospect of the impending triumph of area bombing designed to vaporize whole continents.

The policy of strategic bombing of the primitive sort, aimed at destroying German machinery and German morale, was given its clearest expression and highest blessing by Churchill and Roosevelt at about the time I was polishing my new pair of wings in the beginning of 1943. I had no idea that the President and the Prime Minister, along with their respective chiefs of staff and attendant Brass, were meeting in Casablanca to make short-range plans for what was quite possibly our short-range lives.

The meeting unleashed my commanders to try their hand at winning the war by bombing, although, as a gesture to more conservative military thinking, the Allied leaders specified that the air war was essentially a preparation for the invasion of Europe. However, this could take place only if the Luftwaffe and the industrial machine that kept it running were substantially destroyed.

No matter that in its hour of seeming triumph strategic bombing was still tied to a projected land operation. In the months, perhaps years, before invasion, the Air Forces were to be turned loose under their own commanders. If they could locate and destroy the vital sources of

Hitler's strength the Air Forces would have won the war not only against Hitler but against the Army and the Navy.

The British had come to Casablanca with a well-rehearsed team, supplied with impressively drawn documentation, to argue against the idea of a cross-Channel invasion in 1943. They proposed instead to attack the underbelly of Hitler's Europe from the Mediterranean and to relieve the Russians by intensifying the air war in the west.

Such a policy had already been cleared with the Russians in the preceding August. Those negotions between Churchill and Stalin had been acrimonious. The talk had taken place in the Kremlin. The host had been baiting his guests with such questions as "When are you going to start fighting? . . . Are you going to let us do all the work while you look on? . . . You will find it not too bad once you start. . . ."

Churchill is reported to have exploded, smashed his fist on a table and launched into a lengthy oration on Britain's sacrifices and fighting tradition. Stalin stopped the translator midway and remarked, "I do not understand what you are saying, but, by God, I like your sentiment."

Stalin was mollified not so much by Churchill's passion as by his discussion of the RAF plan to bomb Germany and by the Prime Minister's expressive doodle of a European crocodile exposing its tender belly to the planned thrust from North Africa. The cry for a second front continued, but Stalin seemed to have accepted the intensifying air war as an effective flanking of the enemy.

At Casablanca in January 1943 the Americans were divided among themselves, with the crusty Admiral

Ernest Joseph King stubbornly maintaining that the war had to be fought and won by the U.S. Navy in the Pacific. Sir Charles Portal, Britain's Air Marhsal, compared King's approach to the European war with the "position of a testator who wishes to leave the bulk of his fortune to his mistress. He must, however, leave something to his wife, and the problem is to decide how little he can in decency set apart for her." Roosevelt, who tried, with gentle teasing, to soften the flinty Admiral, was fond of saying that King was so tough he shaved with a blowtorch. Playing upon the President's sentimental loyalty to the Navy, King had been able to sidetrack an urgently recommended proposal by the British Chief of Staff calling for the creation of an Anglo-American force of four to six thousand bombers by April 1944.

The airmen presented a united front in Casablanca. Arnold and Portal saw eye to eye on promoting the air war. Each was afraid that his boss would cave in under pressure from the competing services. Arnold fretted lest Churchill, who had always regarded daylight bombing as probably quixotic and wasteful, would persuade the President to give it up. In the middle of the conference Arnold summoned Eaker, who could be counted upon to bring a touch of front-line reality to the rarefied atmosphere of Casablanca villas bleaching languorously in the sun. Eaker would be the man to ram home the need for planes and crews and money. Churchill would have to be seduced by such rough wooing if the President was to be won.

Eaker had been already needled to a fine point of exasperation. He had a mission to organize an air force and get it off the ground in the shortest possible time on an island which for half a year is wrapped in mist and rain. Moreover, many of the promised planes and crews had been diverted to North Africa, leaving him what he called a "piddling force of Fortresses" with which to win the war.

Eaker arrived in Casablanca late at night. Early the following morning he hurried over to the hotel, some five miles out of Casablanca, where he found his chief shaving.

"Son," said Arnold, "I've got bad news for you." Through the lather he told Eaker of a disastrous luncheon conversation in which the Prime Minister had directly asked the President to discontinue daylight bombing and attach the Eighth Air Force to the RAF for night work.

As Eaker recalls his response in that bathroom interview, he told his chief, "If the directors of this war are that stupid, count me out."

He went on to specify his objections: The Luftwaffe would escape destruction, and therefore any invasion of northern Europe would end in disaster; the Russians would get no relief; American crews were not trained for night flying, particularly in British fog.

The arguments were familiar to Arnold, and the recital constituted a dress rehearsal. The performance would take place with Churchill as audience. Three days later Eaker had his chance. The Prime Minister met him wearing an RAF uniform. (Churchill usually carried with him a variety of uniforms so that he could meet any adversary on his own grounds in the everlasting war of the services.)

Churchill attempted to soothe Eaker as he might a favorite child to whom he had to deny a promised outing. "My mother was an American . . ." he began, using a familiar gambit. He referred to the Americans' "gallant losses," which he said were running far higher than those of the RAF.

Eaker, pleading for a fair hearing, handed him a one-page case for "day bombing." In it he contended that daylight bombing was more accurate, more economical, denied any respite to the Germans, destroyed German day fighters, and complemented the RAF nighttime operations.

Eaker says that Churchill paused when he came to a phrase in the memo: "Bombing around the clock." He remembers that the Prime Minister savored it, which would be heady praise indeed from the war's mightiest phrasemaker. "Bomb the devil round the clock," Churchill murmured. After mulling the memo for a minute the Prime Minister ended the interview by assuring Eaker that, although he remained unconvinced, he would grant Eaker and Arnold more time to prove their case and for the present would withdraw his request that the President change American policy.

The British won almost all their other policy objectives at Casablanca, and there is little reason to doubt that Churchill could have ended the American idea of daylight bombing if he had been determined to do so. Eaker's little phrase of "bombing round the clock," catchy as a show-tune lyric, may well have saved the day for the cause of Billy Mitchell and paved the way for the Schweinfurt experiment.

The resolutions of the conference, drawn up in haste before Churchill went off for a few days to paint the Atlas Mountains, contained the "Casablanca Directive." This stated the purpose of the combined Anglo-American air offensive to be "the progressive destruction and dislocation of the German military industrial and economic system, and the undermining of the morale of the

German people to a point where their capacity for armed resistance is fatally weakened."

Specifically the Eighth Air Force was ordered: "Attack Germany by day, to destroy objectives that are unsuitable for night attack, to sustain continuous pressure on German morale, to impose heavy losses on the German day fighter force, and to contain German fighter strength away from the Russian and Mediterranean theatres of war."

German postwar historians have sought to shift the guilt for terror to the Allies. One of them, Hans Rumpf, notes: "The significance of the Casablanca Directive lies in the fact that it sought to make indiscriminate bombing respectable as a means of waging war . . . the whole of Germany was now declared a target area. . . . It was the Casablanca Directive which first turned the war into a people's war."

Personally I doubt that. Long before the Casablanca Directive, London and Coventry had been blasted, vast populations had been impressed into slave labor, and death camps were beginning to vaporize Jews, dissident Christians, Gypsies and those too gentle in body, mind or spirit to be allowed a role in the New Order. The war needed no license from Casablanca to become an organized onslaught against plain people, which, I suppose, is what is meant by a "people's war."

Shortly after Eaker returned victorious to High Wycombe he was visited by Colonel Perera, who had recorded the first mention of Schweinfurt as a target in his memoranda. He came as part of a delegation from the U.S. Committee of Operations Analysts. The group was of a very elegant mettle, but the financial and industrial community had to be restrained from showing too obvious a hand in the picking of German targets lest their motives be suspect. Secretary of War Henry L. Stimson had tactfully weeded out of the delegation the financier-industrialist Thomas W. Lamont and Elihu Root, whose position as counsel for Pan American Airways might have been misunderstood by English interests who were maneuvering for postwar control of the air bases being readied for us in England.

The committee found Eaker courteous but cool. When he somewhat reluctantly agreed to see the committee he took up most of the time in restating his familiar complaint about the short-changing of the Eighth. His warnings that the committee ought not to bother "overworked" British agencies for "useless information" suggested that he was fobbing them off. On their own the committee nosed about England. They found some of the British target pickers "out of town"—an unassuming phrase used to indicate that they were flying missions to get a firsthand view of the operations they were planning. Colonel Perera put together a preliminary report suggesting that an American daylight assault on Germany might be expected to cost thirty out of a hundred planes, but that "such losses may be accepted where the objective is a vital high-priority target."

Unaware of such odds against them, *Tondelayo*'s crew went on buzzing cows in Iowa.

6

Kimbolton is a squat, spreading castle set down in a park like a dowager at a lawn party. It is called a castle though it has no battlements, no parapets, and no embrasure from which a cannon or a crossbow might be fired. It was once a genteel prison for the proud, sad and somewhat stuffy Catherine of Aragon. In it she died, to the great joy of Henry VIII, who had changed the course of political and theological history to put her on this royal shelf.

When the 379th intruded upon Kimbolton, the castle was being used as a very proper school from whose portico there issued at regular intervals groups of exuberant but mannerly boys in knee pants, blazers, and caps. The airdrome, once an RAF fighter base, had been given longer runways and was otherwise remodeled to fit a bomber's needs. Despite these changes the base was still wholly submerged into the village of Kimbolton, not at odds with the landscape, the streets, the houses or the church, which stood higher and more prominent than the control tower. Nissen huts, pubs, hayricks, hangars, runways and rutted roads awash with springtime mud made up a community that blurred distinctions between military and civilian lives. I found it charming to walk in meadows, smell cow paddies and at the same time hear the roar and swish of aircraft circling like crows over cornfields.

We had come down from Prestwick by stages, stopping first at Bovingdon. There RAF men briefed us on what we might face. They did it with such jocular, offhand humor that I could scarcely pay attention to what they were saying, so beguiled was I with their manner of saying it. The British, I quickly found, play themselves superbly in a nonstop performance. I had been used to watching Americans laugh at their own fears, ridicule them, or shout them down with hilarious mock panic. These British instructors seemed determined to conquer death by patronizing it. It was an elegant approach.

There were navigators' briefings, pilots' briefings and gunners' briefings. One of the axioms suggested by the British declared that only a fool would go over a target twice in the same mission. That advice was actually useless to us; it was meant for the upper echelons who had already formulated their own rules, which would require crews to go around and around as often as need be to put the bombs into the pickle barrel, for that was why we were there. I admired the British for not feeling quite so compulsive about the matter.

On May 19, some twenty crews of the 379th were summoned to a dress rehearsal. While other groups went to Kiel and Flensburg we were to fly a diversion, luring enemy fighters away from the attackers. We took to the air in formation and I thought we were magnificent, stacked like the head of a javelin, weaving white contrails across the heavens. We skirted the coast of Holland, and I fancied the enemy hiding on those gray, hazy islands. We circled to the north, drawing not a single fighter away from the main raiding party, and then came home. I think it was the only time we were to land without so much as a flak hole in *Tondelayo*. It did not count as a mission; it was merely the final touch to our training.

How ready were we for combat? Only once before had the whole group flown in formation and that was out of Fresno, on a junket along the California coast. I do not know how many hours Johnny had at the controls of a B-17, but Bohn had barely twenty. I thought I could navigate well enough, but I supposed that the .50-caliber which swung above my shelflike desk was there largely to ease my nerves and perhaps allow me to express my resentment at being shot at. I suppose it would have been good to give the navigators at least an afternoon of gunnery before combat. It was not to be. The gunners themselves were well trained, I thought. The group command was green. The rule had been that unblooded crews, such as we were, were to be broken in by flying with experienced outfits. But when we came on the scene there was no time for the niceties. Arnold was pushing Eaker to get on with the job.

We were declared fully operational from the moment we landed at Kimbolton. Our ground crews had reached the field only the day before. They had traveled across the States by troop train to New York, where they were marched aboard the ancient *Aquitania*, sister ship of the *Lusitania*, which the Germans had so maladroitly torpedoed before America entered the World War of our parents. The food had been dreadful on the trip over, the ground crews said, and many had to survive on candy bars. The rolling sea was sickening, and the bedbugs were operating in battalion strength.

On the night of our arrival, May 28, the group was alerted. However, we of *Tondelayo*'s crew were stood down, to be saved from battle and kept in reserve. I do not now remember whether there was a reason for our staying home. If Johnny knew of any he told no one. It was not unusual certainly, for some must fight and some must stand by. I remember watching the group go off in the early morning with chipper, overcasual goodbyes. I recall the lonely breakfast and the long wait. They were off to bomb the submarine pens of St.-Nazaire on the southern coast of Brittany where the Loire empties into the sea.

We did not know that 500-pound bombs would bounce off those massive concrete U-boat shelters like Ping-Pong balls. Our predecessors seemed to have effectively wiped out the rest of St.-Nazaire. Admiral Doenitz had already noted: "No dog or cat is left in these towns." There was nothing but the invulnerable submarine pens where Nazi captains slipped in and out coquettishly to lure our bombers to futility or death.

At Kimbolton we spent the day around our tin-roof hut. Six beds lined each long wall. A chest of drawers stood between each pair of beds. Wooden armchairs—of the sort that pass for garden furniture in second-rate mountain resorts—were placed near the two kerosene stoves that took the edge off the springtime chill. Calendar art glorifying the female crotch decorated the walls and the doors. In the evening before, with the heaters glowing and the field mice pattering like rain on the roof, the place had been cozy. There had been twelve of us in the hut—the officers of three crews. Now we tiptoed around the question marks that hung over eight of those beds. The orderly's broom stirred spirals of dust into the sunlight. We watched the sweeping process as if it were an absorbing maneuver.

We went down to the line with the ground crews to watch the others come home. They came not in battle formation but in a straggling line like geese after a shotgun volley. Here and there a flare arched into the overcast to summon fire trucks and ambulances. The group had sent up twenty-four planes—240 men—to bomb those pens. Three crews had aborted. We counted seventeen as they touched down. One plane had been seen to go down under fighter attack over Brittany, and two succumbed to flak over the target. Carlson's plane had been shot up but made it back on two engines to a potato patch seven miles from Kimbolton.

Our own hut was untouched by the day's events. The war had come to other huts, where beds were stripped and made ready for replacements with the swift efficiency which only later we understood to be kind. Thus those who went, went quickly, leaving scarcely a trace. We could then call the war and the Army cruel and feel less guilt ourselves.

Thirteen days went by in that muddy English spring. Replacements arrived to keep us up to strength. My log says we flew two hours on one day, two hours and five minutes on another day, and so on. I cannot now tell why. In any case these exercises served to give me something to do. I etched the pleasant geography of the Midlands on my mind so that I could see a bend of the Ouse and know that I could follow it home. I learned to distinguish Kimbolton's steeple from that of Chipping Norton, to find patterns in forest and tilled field that would serve as signposts. I came to know Kimbolton by such checkpoints the way a dog teaches his nose a private code of smells.

In thirteen days the thirty men our group lost at St.-Nazaire had been buried in some deep grave within us and no longer gave us trouble. It became clear that death in the air was not a heroic fall but swift and total oblivion like the action of an eraser on a blackboard. After all these years I cannot be certain of what I felt then. I remember fear, but I remember more vividly a kind of exultation. I recall the excitement of that inner battle along with the seductions of England and the glory of riding in the sky.

We were alerted on the night of June 10. I think I wrote a letter to my wife, but I cannot now be sure, for it is not among the packets of V-mail curling and discoloring in their carton. Bohn was in the sack reading when I came into the hut. Bob and Johnny came in later. I remember that I fell asleep as I usually do, almost instantaneously. I woke to a flashlight beam in my face, the glare of a bulb overhead and a voice that said, "Briefing at four." I recollect the flow of obscenities that followed with the wistful sentimentality usually reserved for such homey things as the smell of a fire in a hearth or the warmth of a wool blanket on a cold night.

"What son of a bitch was that?" "It's the middle of the motherfuckin' Goddamned night." "Shut the fuckin' door—it's colder 'n a witch's tit." It was the routine indignation, the customary riot of Americans responding to military orders. I liked it then. I like it more in retrospect. I lay a little while, as was—and is—my habit, seeking to come to terms with the day ahead, particularly this day of our first battle. I was never one for leaping out of bed. I must persuade my legs to reach for the floor.

Bob was up and bouncing. He bubbled and yiped like a boy before a picnic. "Benny, get up, you bastard. Gonna sleep all day? Oh, Mama, it's cold." He slung his towel over his shoulder and dashed out toward the latrine, shouting at the moaning forms he left behind him, "Goddamned son of a bitch, get up." It was as innocent, as joyful, as the wag of a tail.

I chose to wash and shave at the mess hall, where there was a modicum of warmth. I dressed and put on a tie. I remember that, and yet it seems a very formal dress for battle. Over it went the thick-ribbed yellowish olive-drab sweater and the coveralls with capacious pockets to hold all sorts of things from rations in case of disaster to spare pencils. (I was always afraid of being caught without a pencil in the heat of battle. It was far more important than my pistol, which I hung from my belt as an ornament like the lieutenant's bars I pinned to my collar tabs.)

The sun was not yet up, but the sky was fading. On the way to the mess hall, amid the hushed sounds of men walking and the clink of mess gear, I rode my bike into a ditch and thought it ignominious, like falling off a horse en route to Armageddon. I startled a bird above me into a squawking takeoff and set some nameless creature to scurrying out of my ditch. I remounted and wobbled my way to the mess.

The coffee was rank and acrid but steaming, and we warmed our hands on the cracked and mottled mugs. "It'll be a milk run," someone said. And someone added grimly, "Like Saint-Nazaire."

I felt myself to be a witness to the scene, nothing more. Yet my spine tingled, so well did we play our parts. I checked my navigator's case inside my musette bag, strapped it over my shoulder, and joined the others strolling from the mess hall. The pale sun had risen and now hung barely visible through veils of cloud. A farmer in heavy boots plodded across the meadow that sloped away from the mess hall. I stared after him as he walked until his shadowy figure merged into the mist that rose like steam. He was part of the hedgerows, the turned furrow and the halting birdsong, but also as much a part of the war as I was.

We climbed onto a truck, one of a line that waited along the pathway. Firefly cigarettes glowed in the dark beneath the canvas, and talk was hushed as if the rest of the world still slept. Someone said the mission would be scrubbed. I do not know how many wished it, though we had to say so lest we seem too heroic. I know that I did not want to go back and sit on my cot, smoke, and unwind the lean, hard tightness in my gut. It was not a heroic lust for battle; I knew I would come back. Only in some well-concealed corner of my brain did I consider those who would die that day.

The truck ground its gears, lurched onto the road and carried us to headquarters, where an MP in gleaming white belt and leggings stood on guard, a little self-consciously. We jammed past him as if he were a potted palm. (The very anticipation of danger confers an utterly outrageous arrogance on a man.)

There was a scramble for seats on the narrow wood benches of the briefing room. The map was still shuttered. The lineup of crews and their positions in formation were still concealed. The Air Forces had an eye for staging and a sense of suspenseful timing, though sometimes they did milk a moment for its drama. We sat as if in school assembly. The death's-head-and-crossed-bombs insignia on our leather jackets and the pistols dangling from our belts lent a boyish wickedness to the scene. On the stage a gawky young S2 captain was peering at us over his glasses. He wore the smile of a schoolmaster who holds the answers to the test questions.

"Tenn—hut," someone called, and we found our feet not with military alacrity but more as in a seventh-inning stretch at a ball game. Colonel Mo, CO, in full flying gear, strode down the aisle, head lowered like a charging bull. He was twenty feet tall and his shoulders were square and wide as the front end of a jeep.

"At ease," the CO said. "Take your seats, gentlemen." He then shrank a bit to near-human size. The intelligence captain at a nod from Mo opened the cabinet doors and pulled aside a white sheet that covered the map of Britain and western Europe. We followed the red woolen line across the blue islands of the Dutch coast down an inlet to Bremen. (Cries, groans, catcalls.)

The S2 captain took up the lesson for the day: The enemy will have 152 flak cannon at the target, but not all can be brought to bear on you at once. (Cries of "Mama, take me home.") On the way in, it would be a good idea to avoid this island here. (With his pointer the lecturer probed the Dutch coast like a nearsighted insect feeling the way with his antenna.) They call it Wanderooge. . . . The enemy can bring to bear on you 97 heavy cannon and 126 light cannon. . . . In the area there is a possible force of 576 FW-190s and about 105 ME-210s. The enemy's radar can probably pick you up before you leave England, so you may catch quite a few fighters up there. . . . If you go down you all have an escape kit on which we briefed you last week. . . . If you do go down, head for Stettin or Lübeck, travel by night and try to contact a fishing boat. (Gales of laughter, and Mo calls for order.) The S2 captain paused, removed his glasses and said, "Good luck," as any teacher might say to any class about to takes its finals.

Lights went out and the projector beamed upon the screen a diagram of cumulus clouds piled layer upon layer. There were wind arrows carrying figures of velocities, estimates of temperature and the visibility at all possible flying altitudes. I scribbled away out of nervousness, though I knew I would pick up a mimeographed summary of it all.

Next on the program were the target blowups. There was a photo of a gray and smoky city. A river which turned out to be the Weser snaked in from the North Sea. Then we saw the secondary target—Wilhelmshaven. It seemed that such naval bases were surrounded by walls of artillery. We were to circle up from the south and plaster Wilhelmshaven if Bremen proved to be invisible. Bremen or Wilhelmshaven—it was all the same to us. For those cities the verdict would depend on the variable winds. If the clouds blew one way Bremen would burn. If they went the other way Bremen would have its lunch hour as usual and Wilhelmshaven would go up in smoke. We—the bombers—were as indifferent as the rain. That is perhaps as close as men may come to gods—totally irresponsible.

The lights came on and Operations Officer Major Rip Rohr in a squeaky voice piped, "All right, you men, the colonel wants to say a few words."

Colonel Mo disdained the platform and the lectern. He rose and waved to the right, whereupon the S2 captain leaped to his feet and swung aside the shutters of the triptych on which was chalked the battle lineup. The group itself would fly high in a formation of some two hundred planes that were to storm Germany. However, our squadron would fly low within the group. *Tondelayo* was slated to be the squadron's deputy leader, to ride outside Carlson's right wing. The briefing room buzzed as each man tried to divine his fate in chalkmarks much as prophets used to study the flight of geese or the entrails of slaughtered sheep. Is a high spot in the formation good or bad? Is it true that Jerry is picking on the high ones, as the fellow said at mess? Or did he say it was the low groups that were getting it? I quite forgot the meaning of the augury.

The colonel held up his hand to stop the speculation. "Gentlemen," he said in a tone which had a solemn ring for all its casualness, "we've come this far to do a job. Let's do a good one. That's all." It was crisp and brassy West Point.

The pilots shambled to their feet and filed out. The bombardiers queued for their target charts. The navigators flocked to another room where Dutch, the group navigator, was sitting crosslegged on a rickety table, reading aloud his computations of headings, winds, ground speeds and airspeeds in a prayerlike drone. At his side lay a stack of flimsies summarizing the data. I took a few notes, picked up a flight plan and admired my set of gorgeous linen maps in aquamarines and blues and browns.

I rummaged through my locker in sudden senseless panic. I was furious when the winding coil of my oxygen mask became absurdly tangled with my holster. I was in a sweat because I feared—in a complete lapse from rationality—that it was later than I thought, though I had just checked my watch in a ceremonious countdown to the ticking tenths of seconds of Greenwich Mean Time. I was terrified that somehow the crew might go without me.

I checked my maps, charts, pencils, oxygen mask. I

swung my pistol over my hip to be out of my way, climbed into my boots, dangled my helmet over my wrist, felt for the dogtags around my neck and my escape kit in my knee pocket, probed yet again for logbook, dividers, again the pencils, gloves—good God, I had forgotten the gloves. And so it went until I hurled it all into a truck and climbed over the tailgate to be driven down the country road. From a rise I could see mist lapping the valley floor. The runway vanished into cloud. When we came to *Tondelayo* I called out to the driver and he swerved dangerously close to the plane's wing. The rest of the crew were already there. Tailgunner Mike and our radioman, Duke, were clad in their sky-blue electric suits with the wires showing like ribs. They looked like cheerful kids at Halloween. Johnny was squatting under the plane chewing a toothpick. Bohn was examining the underside of Number Four engine like a critic at an air show.

I dumped my belongings on the revetment and felt like a very fussy uncle descending with portmanteaus full of encumbrances on a family preparing to climb Mount Everest for a picnic. The crew's smiles were tight, their jokes overly broad, their gestures too casual. They laughed far harder than the jokes merited, and frequently their laughter broke as if they remembered they were in church.

"After today," Duke said, "There's only twenty-four to go."

"There's the jeep." "It's scrubbed—the motherfuckers scrubbed it." "No, no, it's the chaplain." That sad but sensitive man gave us a low-keyed, nondenominational blessing, got back to his jeep, and waved us away.

I ran through the scenario of the upcoming mission with Johnny, who grinned abstractedly, and with Bohn, who didn't smile at all. The rest of the crew gathered around and I told them in general what we would be doing and when.

"Hell," said Leary, our ball-turret gunner. "We'll get back too late for chow. And the fuckin' paddlefeet'll get it all."

"Just so's we get back," said Mike.

Then we climbed into the plane. Our crew chief, Marsden, took a final fond look at *Tondelayo* and turned her over to us like a father entrusting his daughter to a crew of rowdies who had no delicacy at all when it came to handling the anatomy of so sensitive a creature. We waited until the minute hand on our watches spun to the mark laid down in the briefing. With the whine and roar of Number One engine, *Tondelayo* trembled as if on her first adventure. We spiraled upward through the overcast, with wisps of cloud scudding past like dirty gray tatters blown in the wind, until the sun burst upon us, transforming dun to gleaming white in a crystalline sky.

Tondelayo was a bird and I was a clod on her back. I wore over my coveralls, sweater, Mae West and parachute harness, a sandwich board of chain mail, my flak vest. My nose had become the coiled snout of my oxygen mask, which, despite my best efforts at straps and buckles, failed to conform to the rest of my face. "A hard one to fit with a mask," I was told. On my head sat a helmet like an inverted soup bowl. Standing erect in my three pairs of socks and my fleece-lined boots I felt utterly immobilized, but I had only to lower my butt like a lump of lead onto my perch to become part of *Tondelayo*'s mechanism. And so I flew as if her wings were mine.

The undercast broke and I could trace the threadlike canals weaving their complex angular web over the

English fen country. There was a metallic cold in the cabin. When I took my gloves off and touched the grip of my gun the sensation was indistinguishable at first from that of a burn. We followed Colonel Mo up and down over England while the armada assembled. I waited for the minute and the second ordained by our flight plan as the time to leave England.

With twenty-seven minutes to go my head set exploded in a burst of static, and I waited for a question from the cockpit. Instead I heard Duke's beery voice from the radio room: "Sweet A-de-line, my Adeline." Then from the tail, Mike's "Adeline." And from behind the cockpit Larry's high-pitched tremolo: "For you I pine."

Bohn cut in: "What's next on the program?" And Bob said, "Let's have an oxygen check." Suddenly his voice had become brusque, official, a bit edgy: "Bombardier to crew, bombardier to crew, we are at twenty thousand feet. We're having an oxygen check. Come in, tail gunner, come in, tail gunner."

"OK, Bob."

So it went around the plane until it came to me. "Come in, Benny." I looked at Bob. "Dammit," he said. "Come in, Benny."

"I'm standing next to you, Bob. You can see I'm OK, can't you?"

He glared at me with a look that had lost some of its benign innocence. I stared at him uncomprehendingly.

Around and around we went over Great Yarmouth. I could see the planes above and beyond us dipping their wings as they banked in slow turns, their undersides catching the sun. The frost on *Tondelayo*'s plexiglass threw up kaleidescopic fragments of rainbows.

"Why are we turning, Benny? What are we doing, Benny?"

What can I say? "We are circling." They can see that. "We are early, that's all." I feel obliged to be reassuring. "Everything is OK." It is pleasant, this wheeling in the sun like a flock of birds. I am warmed. The sound of the engines is reassuring and I am surprised to find myself sleepy. Am I a cat curled on the seat of a car? Or am I on my way to battle?

Within twenty seconds of our timetable we came up to Great Yarmouth from the southwest and headed out to sea. "Navigator to whoever wants to know. We're leaving the coast."

There was a chorus of "Roger" and bits of bravado. I did not hear Johnny, but I imagined his secret smile.

I announced our position as safely over water so that everyone could test-fire his gun. Before the "Rogers" came in, the guns answered for the gunners. The tail guns chattered as if they were in another county. The belly turret provoked a slight tremor at my feet. I did not pay much mind to the waist guns, but the top turret, firing forward over the cockpit and the nose, burst the air and left us gasping. Bob's guns shook the nose as a dentist's drill rattles one's head. And I joined in the celebration with my own little rattler.

The odor that came from the spent shells and the smoking breech was pungent. That spice is in my nose now though its recollection is burdened with associations that accumulated later. On that virginal June morning it was an aroma gaudy as a striped bow tie, zestful as brine in a pickle barrel. I must have been supremely innocent to divorce it from the knowledge of death.

After the test firing we fell into an intense silence louder than the engine noise, louder than the guns. Ahead and above us the armada on dress parade let fly

97

vapor trails like royal plumes. Mechanical things when they are grand as plumed fortresses flashing in the morning become endowed with divine invincibility.

The cold at 25,000 feet, our bombing altitude, penetrated through the fleece and wool to the toes. A chill crept up my sleeves and fastened icy fingers around my ribs. I checked and rechecked the course I would take if we had to fly home. When I felt secure in my mind that at that particular moment I knew precisely where we were and could get from there to anywhere else, I turned to scraping frost from my window. It curled beneath the plastic blade of my plotter and fell in crinkly chunks on my desk. Bob turned and pointed toward the plotter. I handed it to him and he went to work on his windows with a ferocity that seemed to me to verge on the desperate. He was using his whole arm in quick jabs, scratching as if each inch of frost might conceal the enemy. And, indeed, his desperation was more rational than my detachment, for behind the frost there might have been the silhouette of an FW or an ME and it could have meant death.

I recall that not the hazard of fighters but only the penetrating cold seemed real to me—that and the second hand of my watch spinning imperviously. I warned the cockpit several minutes ahead, of the time and degree of our turn. When I saw the lead group bank and swing from shadow into sun I scribbled the second into the log. On the horizon in the milky haze of morning fog I saw a shape materialize out of the water. It was Wanderooge. If we went over it there would be flak, according to the notes I had made at our morning lecture.

I pressed my mike button. "Europe up ahead. Hold on to your hats."

My own steel hat weighed painfully. I took it off to

gain a moment's respite, but Bob again sent me a look of rage that bewildered me, and tapped his own helmet furiously. I made placating gestures and put the pot on my head again.

The interphone crackled: "Flak at six o'clock." I noted it and unslung my gun so that it hung free in my hand. Little black clouds materialized up ahead and tore themselves into ugly tatters. I felt the whoosh and, as *Tondelayo* reeled and plunged, I heard the *ping, ping, ping* like pebbles on a metal roof. I realized with a sense of shock that these were shrapnel fragments beating at the shell that held us 25,000 feet above the flatlands of Germany. The flak was coming from Cuxhaven, I thought, and I noted that as absolute fact. We were perhaps a little off course. I could see the Weser as it wound south of Bremerhaven, off the starboard wing, guiding us to Bremen.

A squawk from someone: "Fighters at nine o'clock." I rested my gun on the desk to note developments and saw that the gun was making a grease puddle on the log and the maps. The word "fighters" scrawled its way through the stain.

The convulsion of the turret gun blasting over my head filled the nose. I stopped writing and picked up my gun. The fighters coming in were each an inch of silver against the blue. They came in three abreast at eleven o'clock above the frosty patterns on the port-side window. The wings grew to two or three inches and touched off little sparklers. Then they were no longer inches but massive aircraft, flipping over, spitting, and sliding down out of my gunsights, like gulls gliding down currents of air to the dull metallic sheen of the distant earth.

I pulled the trigger and sent a long burst into space.

Tondelayo, in evasive action, seemed to jump and fall so that much of the time I was standing in air seeking to steady myself on the handlebars of my gun.

My charts were on the floor along with the dividers, the plotters and the other paraphernalia. I noted that we were flying straight on course. I noted the time that had elapsed from the turn into Germany. Cartridge shells littered the nose, and when I moved my feet I slipped on them. When I slipped I swore. When I swore I could feel the sweat on my forehead and marveled that a man could sweat and freeze simultaneously. In the close quarters of our plexiglass cabin, the sting of gunpowder and perhaps the smell of a fart mingled in my nostrils.

If you fly south from the coast of Germany on a course that takes you over Nordholz at a speed of 250 miles an hour you get to Karlshofen in about ten minutes. We of *Tondelayo*'s crew who are still in a position to speak of it think of that run as taking several hours. Karlshofen was our initial point from which we would begin our straight-and-level bomb run to Bremen perhaps six minutes away. At Karlshofen it was quite obvious that we would not see Bremen that day. A bank of thick clouds, rising like mountains out of snowy plains, stretched before us. The armada wheeled and headed westward. Bremen would be spared.

Those unreal fighters, beautiful as swift arrows, came at us again in twos and threes. When a gunner called out from the waist or the tail or the belly turret that he had got one, I logged it for his record, but I couldn't say that I saw an enemy actually downed. From my vantage point I saw them only when they came head on, flashing, turning and exiting in marvelous choreography. The impersonal quality of the menace was eerie. It was as if I were in battle with beautiful birds of prey. I fired my gun and saw the tracers arch toward them inflicting no damage, causing no pain.

I saw death long before I saw pain, and I could not believe it. I balanced my gun in one hand and stared beyond it at Carlson's left-wing man. Was it Johnson? Was it Ashley? I no longer remember. There was a yellow flare on the outboard engine nearest me. The great silver ship banked sharply and turned its belly to the sun, which paled the yellow flames. There were no screams. The plane lost speed, slipped back and spiraled gently down. I saw a piece of wing shatter and fly off like a target in skeet shooting. The broken wing was jagged and flaming. The plane turned tail up, plummeted past my gun port and was no more.

A jangling splutter on my head set: "Plane going down." I acknowledged the report and noted it. I observed the time, place and altitude of each event in an indecipherable scrawl stained with grease and powder marks.

Silently planes were peeling out of that German sky and twisting past my window. I stood on tiptoe to follow them down. In the arctic chill my forehead dripped sweat onto my brows and my nose. I had just pulled aside the elephantine hose of my oxygen mask to tally the dimly seen curves of the Weser with those on my map when I heard an unfamiliar noise like the crunch of metal. Simultaneously I felt that someone had brushed against my helmet, knocking it slightly awry.

White fleecy cotton padding was fluttering around me as if a playful cat had ripped a pillow. Bob turned to me, and his eyes above his mask were clouded with concern. I waved cheerily, then followed his eyes to a jagged hole in the metal frame beneath my window. There *Tondelayo*'s skin had curled inward. I looked behind me

101

to where the cat had ripped the pillow and followed the bullet's course to where it exited above and behind me into the wadding that cushioned the bulkhead. Bob gestured to my helmet and I let my fingers trace the bullet's path in the groove that now creased the tin.

It had been too dreamlike, too bizarre, to stir much fear, but if I had followed that bullet's path still farther into the cockpit I would have been afraid. What happened there I found out from Bohn Fawkes decades later when he and I were reconstructing that first battle from scraps of logs, letters and notes.

Johnny had been at the controls since takeoff. Having no gun, Bohn had taken along a camera, thinking that at least he would record the battle if he could not play a bigger part. He had been snapping shots of fighters as they came at us. He was trying to focus when the FW-190 sent its 20-mm. shells to puncture *Tondelayo*'s nose. The shell that creased my helmet went on to pass through Johnny's rudder pedal, missing his foot narrowly as it had missed my head. Johnny yelled and clutched Bohn's thigh in a signal to take over. Johnny's eyes, alight with panic, were signal enough. Bohn dropped his camera, gripped the wheel and thought no more of Johnny's eyes. Holes were opening in the group's formation, but there was still a semblance of order in the ranks as we started our run to Wilhelmshaven. What happened as we passed over those flatlands was not clear to us at the time. The rear ranks of a parade have no idea of why the line up ahead may waver. They do not know that men have dropped down and others must step over or around them, disturbing the tempo of the march, violating the rectilinear precision of the files as one might rip the fabric of a flag.

We saw only that Colonel Mo's ship was swooping to

left and right, describing S turns in the sky, and that the 379th, in trying to follow him, was falling into a formless rout. We did not know that the lead plane of the group ahead of us had two of its engines blasted by flak and had slowed to a crawl over that landscape from which came bomb bursts and legions of Focke-Wulfs and Messerschmitts.

Mo was trying to avoid overrunning the group ahead of him. We were trying to avoid overrunning Mo, and so the group disintegrated. Battles had not been fought in tidy formations since the Crimean War, but we had been taught that strict formation flying was as vital to us as the British square had once been to the infantry. Not for us the anarchic whooping attack en masse. To be uncovered by a formation's friendly fire was to be naked and next to dead.

Seeing our ragged line zigzagging on a bomb run, the enemy came at us like wolves after straggling sheep. We had moved in so close to Colonel Mo that our wing tip was almost within reach of his waist gunner. Bohn had never flown formation at high altitudes. Johnny was an experienced formation flyer, but he was sitting on an unexploded 20-mm. shell somewhere in his seat and the thought paralyzed him.

Bohn's tactic was to follow Mo as a chick follows its mother. We were tucked in so tight that our spent shells bounced off the wings of a B-17 beneath us. We could see that in the low group there was not a single plane that did not have at least one feathered prop.

When we came to a wide bay we saw the German smoke pots cloaking our target, Wilhelmshaven. Out of the smoke rose a storm of flak, rocking *Tondelayo*, sending fragments through its metal skin, biting into her delicate electric nerves.

I called out the heading for the target, but Bob was already on top of his sight. We could not bomb as a group but only in train, following the plane ahead, hoping to hit the submarine pens we could not see. The explosions billowed up above the veil of smoke, but we could not be sure of whether we were plastering the shipping, the bay, the harbor or the bistros, whorehouses, shops and homes of Wilhelmshaveners.

I had worked out a course for home, straight across the Helgoland Bight to the open sea and then on a dogleg to England.

Once we got past the archipelago that guarded Germany's North Sea coast, the fighters left us. We drew together in formation as geese do. No one on *Tondelayo* was wounded. But the plane itself had been riddled, and the hydraulic line was cut so that we had only mechanical brakes.

I took off my helmet and studied the crease in it. My hair was damp with sweat, but my shoulders shook with the chill. The wind made a whistling sound through the shell hole. When we dropped below fifteen thousand feet I tore the mask from my face, breathed freely and felt oddly exhilarated. At twelve thousand feet I told the crew they too could take off their masks. As we came in low over Kimbolton several planes in the group were firing their flares to call the ambulances. Bohn brought the plane down on the runway and then taxied onto the grass where our brakes might hold.

I gathered my equipment, my charts and my smudged, filthy log and dropped a bag full of the stuff through the hatch to the grass. Then I jumped out and took a turn around *Tondelayo* to see her scars. Mike was telling us how the fighters came in at the tail, and I was assuring him that I had noted his kill claims. Johnny came out long after the rest of us. He had part of the torn cockpit seat in one hand and his parachute in the other. He and Bohn had been looking for the shell and had found it in the silken folds on which Johnny sat. He held it up like an angler with a prize fish, and Bohn snapped a picture of it. Then we tore the parachute to pieces to make the scarves we fancied.

Johnny said little then, but that was not surprising. None of us said much. I interpreted the blots and grease stains on my log to an intelligence officer at the debriefing while pouring hot coffee down my throat.

On the way back to my hut I saw a man and a woman watching us. We stared at each other across the field. They waved, and we waved back. What had they done for the past six hours? They had killed no one. They saw no one die. They were coming home from work and so were we.

Among the critics of warfare who study the final tally sheets, the morning had been interesting but less than sensational. Our losses were reckoned as slight: only eight of the 168 that the Eighth Air Force had sent against Germany that morning, an eminently acceptable rate of loss. But of that eight, six were from the 379th, and of that six, four were from our 527th Squadron, leaving only two crews alive and home at the end of the day though we were six when we started. That was a loss of 66.6 percent, and some of us began to calculate our odds for survival on that basis.

Even though *Tondelayo*'s crew had lost no blood there was a silent, invisible hemorrhage that was beyond the healing power of our flight surgeon, who, in any case, turned out to be an obstetrician.

7

We of *Tondelayo*, obsessed with our own close shaves and vanished friends, gave little thought to the deplorable, disorderly scattering of our bombs over Wilhelmshaven. We realized that it was a botched job, but we gave ourselves some credit for bringing back one plane and one crew. That was an achievement which consoled us mightily.

However, judging by the painful message from General Arnold to General Eaker concerning the battle, our survival was of distinctly less comfort to our troubled chiefs. Hap Arnold, in icy tones, had complained of the result and asked his good friend but military subordinate why only 250 crews could be assembled for a major battle. "I realize that when you lose a plane over Germany the crew goes with it," Arnold had cabled. "But I cannot accept the fact that when a plane is shot up the whole crew is knocked out. There must be some salvage and from this salvage we should be able to make up crews that can operate."

It was on that occasion, I believe, that Eaker went out to the nearest combat base and found a B-17 with a hole in the wing—not a very difficult thing to find in those days. He had himself photographed with his head sticking up through the wing and sent a print to Arnold, captioned "We didn't send this one back today."

He says it was the closest he came to being sacked by his friend. The story fed the legend of Eaker's scrappiness.

We salvaged ourselves as best we could in the days following Wilhelmshaven. Our ground crew, under the resourceful Marsden, scrounged supplies and parts from other craft to patch *Tondelayo*. In the same way new men were found to restore the squadron. Names were selected from lists of unattached arrivals, and in time these names and numbers materialized into men carrying parachute bags and assorted bits of flight gear, flopping on vacant beds, filling dresser tops with snapshots of new women.

Much of the salvage was invisible and highly personal. Each of us rebuilt his self-image to incorporate the battle of Wilhelmshaven. As I look upon the young man who allegedly was I in that wartime spring I find him almost a tourist although an enthusiastic one, reveling too much in the experience, perhaps. I believe he was reconciled to the blood of others but not his own. A secure childhood fosters a belief in one's immortality.

Bob, my companion in *Tondelayo*'s nose, was a riotous put-on in those early days. I was gulled into thinking he was unshaken beneath his armor of innocence. I think now that perhaps it was I who wore such armor.

Johnny, our pilot in chief, hid behind his cowboy

mask. To me at least, he was a cartoon character with a balloon ascending from his mouth reading in exclamatory type, "Aw shit."

He did not talk about the unexploded shell that had landed in the parachute. He scarcely talked at all, as I remember. I thought at the time that he had set a distance between himself and me, but I have learned since that he was no closer to Bohn, with whom he shared the cockpit and who, to their mutual embarrassment, was an inevitable albeit discreet witness to his sufferings.

Two days after Wilhelmshaven we set out for another try at Bremen. There was a briefing in the middle of a chill, dark night, and we rallied in a chillier dawn over the marshlands of Lincolnshire, then headed again for the shipyards of north Germany. It was over the North Sea that Johnny went on the intercom to ask me for a heading home. I no longer remember the complaint. Perhaps Johnny did not like the whine of an engine as we climbed. I myself cannot read the subtleties of motor noises.

We slipped back from formation, dropping to a lower altitude. We were alone between sky and sea. The enemy still waited along the coast. I corrected course to avoid British flak and headed for Kimbolton. Once on the ground, Johnny had to explain the abort to Marsden, who took the accusations concerning *Tondelayo*'s behavior as a reflection on his care for her. The rest of us groused in our huts, wrote letters and again turned up on the line like bystanders to watch the boys come home.

Our group had made it to Bremen, and other groups had gone to Kiel, but again the results were less than encouraging, the cost exorbitant. To make matters worse for our high command, many of the crews had been caught cleaning their guns over the North Sea on the way home, impotent as ducks, when German fighters zoomed out of dazzling sunlight and riddled plane after plane. In all, twenty-six crews went down that day, and poor Ira Eaker had a bad time accounting for them to Arnold.

On the following day under heavy skies we rode over the Midlands to check out an engine. On the day after that we were off to France. It was to have been a milk run. And it might have been, but again *Tondelayo* sounded a discordant note in Johnny's ears. Once again we fell from formation and he called for a heading home.

Bob was furious and no fit company in our nose compartment. We had had all the agonies of anticipation, the burdens of preparation and the hazards of a lone flight back. And we were no nearer the magic number of twenty-five than if we had slept in the sack all day anesthetized to war. After we landed, Mike and Duke resumed a card game in the barracks. Bohn shrugged. Larry, our engineer, who must have been as sensitive as Johnny to *Tondelayo*'s delicate condition, looked pained. I wrote a letter to my wife remarking that it was a pity that since we were not fighting I had to be deprived of London.

June was bright and pleasant that year. There were few days on which clouds grounded us. The sun warmed the grass to a soft, sweet smell. The mud in the lanes had hardened into a dry powder except in the field where I went to pick a poppy. There it still lapped over the toes of my high-laced GI shoes.

On June 22 we went on the first daylight raid over the Ruhr. We were to visit the I. G. Farben Industrie Chemische Werke in Huls, which had been making 3,900 tons of synthetic rubber every month, much of it going to the nearby Buna tire factory. Huls had been almost untouched by war since 1941 when the RAF raided it by night.

Our main force, 183 bombers, was to head for the familiar North Sea archipelago, feint toward Bremen or Wilhelmshaven, then abruptly swing southeast to the Ruhr. Simultaneously a smaller diversionary force was to go to Antwerp. The British were off to Amsterdam, and a fledgling group of B-17s were assigned to confuse the enemy by flying mysteriously out over the North Sea. It was hoped, the professorial intelligence captain told us, that most of the German fighters would either be buzzing over the North Sea ports or swarming over Belgium, leaving the Ruhr to us.

The plan worked out rather well. It would have worked still better if the Antwerp contingent had been on time. As it was, the German flight dispatchers spotted us heading toward Germany's heart before they could be distracted by the decoys over Belgium.

Though the fighters found us, the flak was not nearly as bad as we had expected. Certainly we rocked with the bursts and *Tondelayo*'s hide was punctured, but not in any vital area. We found out later that the sheer audacity of our mission had saved us. Apparently the Germans refused to believe that American bombers would ever fly over the Ruhr in broad daylight.

The I. G. Farben workers came into the streets of Huls at the sound of our engines to marvel at what they took to be an air show put on for their amusement and for the glory of the Reich. No alarm wailed; no antiaircraft guns were fired. There was only the distant drone of our armada flying high.

In ten minutes we killed 186 astonished people and wounded a thousand more. Some of our bombs scored near-misses on two air-raid shelters. The impact, however, was enough to crack the shelter walls and bury ninety more who had taken cover.

At the time we did not know or try to guess how many people we might have killed that morning in Huls. Now I sometimes try to cloak that skeletal arithmetic with flesh. It is as impossible as it was to discern a human smile in the smoke that curled from the chimneys of a crematorium. I recall only the smoke that came up from Huls almost to our heaven.

We fought our way to the coast against persistent attacks, but what I remember mainly about that mission was the comforting spectacle of Spitfires and Thunderbolts rising to greet us as we reached the sea. Then the FW's and the ME's faded away. We dropped lower, ripped off our masks, breathed and relaxed as if we had finished a hard day's work. And so we had, exploding something into nothing.

Our losses, including those of the main and diversionary forces, amounted to twenty planes, two hundred men, roughly ten percent. Nevertheless, our superiors were pleased with us because we had dropped 422 tons of bombs and, according to the reconaissance photos, only 333.4 tons had been wasted on homes, streets, public parks, zoos, department stores and air-raid shelters. This passed for precision.

Actually Huls might have been put out of commission permanently if there had been a follow-up. After our mission the city went almost unscathed right to the end of the war. We had devastated buildings and shaken morale, but tire production, although on a limited scale, was resumed within a month. Synthetic-rubber production suffered perhaps six months but soon was reaching new peaks.

I have searched the records and find no explanation for our failure to return and finish the job. The Germans were astonished at the time. After the war American scholars of our air strategy were surprised, but nobody nitpicks a victory. A cold analysis of the balance sheet at Huls indicates that the lives lost that day—American and German, in the air, on the ground and in shelters underground—had not brought closer the end of the war or of Hitler. But at the time we did not know the price and thought we had a bargain.

We gathered in the officers' club we called Duffy's Tavern. The presiding spirit, whose name we could scarcely remember before it became Duffy, was a likable man. His wartime job was honorable and his rank was not excessive if one considers the exalted station sometimes given to errand boys who man desks at headquarters. Duffy was one of a number of men who resigned from combat without losing the affection of his comrades. Such an attitude may sound bizarre to civilians or to soldiers made of sterner stuff than we were, but men who have been in combat ought to be the first to understand fear.

Major Culpepper was more likely to occasion resentment because he flew combat but with a fastidious eye to the relative safety of the missions he chose for himself. His executive duties in the group always interfered with his flying if the mission was over Germany, if the escorts were insufficient, or if the group's position in the wing seemed likely to prove excessively hazardous. He became known as the "Milk-Run Major" and his name was welcomed on the battle roster as a sure sign of an easy day.

Those days were rare that summer, and the Major chalked up only a few missions. Perhaps I am unkind to him. I do not know his private agonies or his fierce obsession with personal survival. I think that such a passion may be the key to his character and to the characters of many others who resigned from combat. They had an overriding personal necessity to preserve their bodies intact. It is hard to argue against such an order of priorities. Cool logic is not equal to the task.

I know a little more about Snuffy, because he flew with us for a while that summer. It was after our third mission, as I recall, that he made up his mind to survive. In refusing to fight he stood his ground with indomitable spirit. He was a waist gunner. For three raids he had withstood the numbing cold. He had seen other gunners die and other crews vanish. One summer morning when we were not alerted Snuffy went to see the squadron CO. Our tail gunner, Mike, went with him and so could tell us precisely what happened.

Snuffy saluted with that casual wave to the forehead that was our bow to protocol. "I ain't aflying anymore," he said in his own blend of Kansas and Oklahoma accents.

"What's wrong?" asked Carlson.

"I'm ascared," said Snuffy. "That fuckin' flying's for keeps. I'm agoing to the kitchen."

At that point, Mike says, Snuffy began to tear his sergeant's stripes from his sleeve by way of emphasizing the finality of his decision and his acceptance of the consequences. Theoretically, of course, he might have been given far worse than a demotion—anything from a dishonorable discharge to time in a stockade. The firing squad was, of course, unthinkable. But Snuffy knew that the Army Air Forces were not the Army, that the wartime Army was not the peacetime Army, that his superiors could be trusted to play the game with a sense of proportion if not of humor.

Carlson put up a premonitory hand and tried to be understanding. "I know how you feel," he said. "We're all scared."

"Yup," said Snuffy. "Only me, I'm agoin' to the kitchen."

Snuffy won. He went to the kitchen. He may have been busted to corporal, but I'm not absolutely certain of that and Mike can't remember.

Mike commented to me years later, "It took a lot of guts on his part to admit that he was scared shitless." Mike compared Snuffy to a waist gunner on another crew who took off his gloves and deliberately froze his fingertips in the slipstream at forty below. He was medically grounded after that. He kept his stripes and played hero to the women of Bedford. Mike had no tolerance, even decades later, for those who cohabited with their fear in secret, treating it like a back-street mistress. Those who embraced their fear in public, who vowed to live with it forever and scorned to put on the pious look of heroes, were accepted as Snuffy was in the kitchen and as Duffy was at the bar.

Johnny was different. Johnny thought he was a hero. He hated his fear. He could also count on inertia, the soldier's indispensable resource, which can be stronger than moral or political conviction, and a more significant ingredient of valor than the intoxicant of honor. In that year of 1943 as, I suppose, in all years of all wars, men were able to go from mission to mission to the bitter end—either the glorious finale of orders home or a flaming fall—only because one battle succeeded another as inevitably as the progress of clocks and calendars. It

115

is easier to walk to one's doom in company and in cadence than to step out of line to stand alone, exposed and naked.

Inertia might have won for Johnny, making him a hero in spite of himself, if he had not been in command. After all, I and others like me had no such temptation as those that beset Johnny. I could calculate a course to Kimbolton at any point and pass the appropriate heading to the cockpit, but the plane would not turn back. Its engines would continue to whine and roar and carry us to those dreary cloudscapes where death lay waiting. But Johnny could call for a homeward heading and I would give it to him. With his own hand he could point *Tondelayo* to Kimbolton and safety. With his own ears he could hear the fault in the engine that would serve as an excuse for a reprieve, and who was to contradict him? It is easy enough to be chaste when no temptress is on hand to trip you up and beat you to the ground.

Fear was part of the furniture in every hut, in every pub, in every parlor, bedroom and bath in England, but it was not a grisly rattling skeleton. It did not claw at one's guts. When the fear was light and transient it drove some of us to the palliative of sex. When it was more troubling it provoked a throbbing headache in the back of the neck or hives or flatulence.

I walked the streets of Bedford with an English girl who lived with fear but not as Johnny did. She was married to it. It was her fate which she shared with all Bedford, all England, all the world. We walked past fenced-in fields of rubble and she would tell me who had once lived there. Her reminiscences were spoken in flat tones as if she were recollecting the price of eggs in years gone by.

I had seen her first at a Saturday-night party in the

officers' club when she was one of a group of girls shipped up in a GI truck like a load of powdered eggs. They were all proper girls from proper homes. They were to be used for dancing and to be held vertically for light love only. But their laughter tinkled from the barracks in the summer night. Eventually an order came down from Colonel Mo which read: "All ladies attending Saturday night dances at the Officers' Club MUST be off the base by 0800 Monday morning." Some of the girls, with rumpled hair and heavy-lidded, lustrous, morning eyes, would kiss the boys goodbye before a mission. It was not good for security, but it was pleasant for morale.

Joyce was painfully thin. Her dress hung in a tasteless straight line from her shoulders with scarcely a notice of her young flat breasts. Her nails were long and painted in an electric shade. Her face was pinched, but her smile and her green eyes were warm. I would not now be able to recollect her quite so well if I had seen her only on that one night when she was delivered for our dancing pleasure.

I saw her again at a pub in Bedford. I had gone out to the stone labyrinthine urinal to pee and test my dizziness by looking at the stars. They went around and around as expected. Giddily I thought that the next day might be flyable and possibly fatal.

Piano players in clubs and pubs were still merrily jingling the tunes of our fathers' war: "The bells of hell go ting-a-ling-a-ling for you but not for me." The rhyme danced in my addled, happy mind as I floated back through the blackout curtains of the pub into a blue tobacco fog. Somebody's teary, beery voice was singing a song I cannot now remember, nor ever could.

I took and held her scarlet-tipped hand, thin and fragile as a gazelle's fetlock. Her blond hair fluffed in my nose. When the barmaid pleaded and commanded, "Time, please, glasses please," I held her coat while she missed her sleeves. Outside we wrapped ourselves into each other and kissed. How ardent could I have been with the stars turning slowly, methodically, this way, then that? I now recall not Joyce so much but the moon lighting the houses and enfeebling the little yellow gleams that escaped beneath the blackout curtains of the fish-and-chips shop over the road, the shout of a GI far away and muted like an operatic shepherd's call off-stage, the heavy wooden tramp of a British soldier's boots, and a girl's uneasy laugh. Was it Joyce who laughed or another girl in another's arms? I do not know nor ever did.

She told me I was strange for an American. I was not in such a hurry. I think I said that until that moment I hadn't planned to go anywhere. We talked of this and that, and at some time that evening she mentioned the scrapbook that was to prove relevant to all that I am now recalling of the war in England and of fear.

I remember that I took her home and kissed her as we stood in her doorway. Then I found a GI truck with cigarettes flaring in the dark beneath the canvas. At the curb a soldier vomited. In the doorway of a church a GI had his girl up against the chipped and ancient fieldstone.

"Have a drink, Lieutenant," someone said. "Pardon me, dammit, Lieutenant, I gotta piss. Hold the truck."

When the last man hoisted himself swearing into the dark, the starter whined, the motor caught, the truck roared out its power into the moonlit streets. The breeze that came in over the tailgate caught the embers of the cigarettes and brought in the smell of the meadow. We passed houses asleep and haystacks in the fields ranged like hats on a shelf.

The men counted the drinks, critiqued the screwing and the puking and the hangovers to come. Then the chatter subsided to desultory grunts and snores until an MP's flashlight probed the recesses of the truck. Beyond the sentry we saw the semi-oval entrances of Nissen huts looking like caves in blackness.

I scraped my shins over beds and chairs until I found my cot. Bohn, recognizing my style of floundering, said, "Early briefing." And so I fell asleep.

Another day I walked with Joyce through Bedford, and again her dry recital of the ruins of her neighbors moved me. We came to her house, for she had brought me home to dinner, to see her family and her famous scrapbook.

The table near a bay window was set with ornate silverware on a white cloth. In the center stood a vase of flowers. Mrs. Wofford's thin pale hands toyed with them incessantly while she talked. Her dark-brown hair spread out from the tight confines of her hairdo and hung in strands about her face. Like Joyce she had a peculiarly pinched quality as if the molder of her features had taken a lump of clay and, with thumb and forefinger, formed a ridge, then depressed her cheeks away from her cheekbones. The strain of that rigorous sculpting had remained with Mrs. Wofford.

When Mr. Wofford came in, Joyce disentangled her coltish legs from beneath her and sprang up, all limbs and fluttering bits of organdy, skirting the cluttered room to throw herself about her father's neck. We talked of America and the war, of the Regent's Park Zoo, of my wife and my parents, of what I did before and what I

119

would do after, if there was an after. So it went until the dishes were cleared away. Then Mr. W. picked up the evening paper and Mrs. W. went in to do the dishes. Joyce and I arranged ourselves on the sofa with the scrapbook opened on her lap.

The first pages were devoted to the royal family. There were the official portraits of King, Queen and the little princesses. There they were again at a garden fete and yet again out riding. There was Princess Elizabeth pitching hay. Was Joyce a little girl playing with paper cutouts, and, if so, what had I been up to, kissing her open lips?

The rotogravure pictures were carefully mounted on large yellow pages. On one page there was a meticulously copied portrait of Elizabeth done by Joyce.

She leafed through the pages until she came to those that were filled with photos of boys and young men. Some were grave-eyed with straight, unsmiling mouths as if posing for ceremonial portraits. Some were older, their faces more relaxed. They all wore either an overseas hat perched precariously over one eyebrow or else a peaked cap with the RAF's embroidered bird and crown. All of them were flyers. Scrawled in ink in the corners of the snapshots were sentiments of varying degrees of ardor. Beneath each was inscribed a day, a month, a year, as on a tombstone, occasionally bordered with a penciled pattern of leaves and hearts, like a child's valentine.

Her father went on reading his paper. Her mother stood before us with her hands pink from the dishwater. I had the impulse to slam shut the scrapbook before Mrs. W. could see that private graveyard that her daughter tended. Joyce pointed to one young man. "I loved him best," she said and sighed as if for a pop star. I found it hard to believe that the Woffords could see their daughter in her garden of dead lovers and not weep or rave.

"I've so wanted Joyce to go on with her ballet lessons," said Mrs. Wofford. "But now . . ."

We talked of a weekend Joyce and I might spend in London. "She hasn't been out much lately," said her mother as if she were discussing a breath of air on a Sunday promenade. Then I felt for the first time the fear that lay over England. It was not a fear of dying in a war but of living in an endless war.

Like all England, Bedford waited supinely for death that might come at any time by happenstance. There was nothing to be done about it but smoke one's pipe, read the paper, have a pint. In peacetime too, people died sweetly in bed or nastily under the wheels of a berserk truck. They endured the violent wrench of death quietly or in agony, but the world never stopped.

Unlike the people of Bedford, *Tondelayo* actively sought its fate. Or at least it so appeared. In fact, though, we were swept along as powerless as they. Only a few of us did anything about it. Culpepper the Milk-Run Major, Duffy, Snuffy had said no to war, generals and death. The suspicion now mounted that Johnny was joining that band of determined survivors. I cannot say—nor can any others of the crew—whether Johnny made his decision consciously weighing life against death, any kind of life against any kind of death.

Three times we set out in formation and each time before we hit the enemy coast Johnny asked me dryly, unemotionally, without explanation, for a heading home. We grumbled. Bohn and our engineer, Larry, who witnessed Johnny's decision, shrugged and said nothing. Bob seethed. What was there to do? I didn't think we could talk with him. Johnny would only put his head to

121

one side, chew on a toothpick and walk away.

Bob was not a man to wrap himself in virtue. He was no hero, or at least he thought he wasn't. He wanted desperately to reach that magical number of twenty-five, to go home and pray that the war would end before he was called upon to do another tour. He was in a game and he had to score twenty-five. Johnny was making it difficult.

I thought that Johnny could not go on like this forever. Ultimately he would see that war, even death itself, cannot be cheated. I do not now remember all that I thought. I do know that when Bob spoke, his anger touched off no sparks in me. I think I tried to placate him. But anything that I might have said would seem foolish in retrospect. Bob charged that Johnny was a danger to the crew. Perhaps he was, but I could not think of joining the outcry against him.

It was Bob and Mike and some of the gunners, I believe, who went to Carlson. They wouldn't fly with Johnny, they said. He was going to abort and abort and the crew would never go home.

Were the charges true? How can one be certain that those motor aberrations that Johnny heard were in fact no more than echoes of the fear he shared with all of us? And how could he, himself, distinguish between such phantom noises—if that is what they were—and actual malfunctions in *Tondelayo*, portending real disaster?

Years later I asked Bohn why he wasn't on the delegation, and he asked me the same. "Perhaps," he said, "it seemed to me disloyal." The plain fact was that Bohn could not bear to suggest to himself or to others that he had climbed into the command of *Tondelayo* by stepping on Johnny's neck. Bohn held his soul in his hand and studied it. He feared that he might see in himself not the pure motive of the conscientious officer but the ambition of the mutineer. He stepped aside and let the events transpire that would remove Johnny and open the way for his own succession. And if things did not work out just that way, if Johnny stayed in command, Bohn would have accepted that fate too, his honor intact.

I had no such good excuse. I told Bohn I could understand his abstention but not my own. He thought that I too had not wanted to appear disloyal to Johnny. Maybe so, maybe not. At this distance I cannot be sure. I had no great affection for Johnny, but no reason to dislike him. Perhaps I did not trust my own sentiments any more than Bohn did his. I think I was bemused by the drama of it. In any case, I shrugged and let it happen.

I lay on my bunk and watched Bob's fury after the last abort. I saw him stalk off for his talk with Carlson. It was the responsible thing to do. That I knew even at the time, and in retrospect I can applaud it all the more. The motive of the rebels may have been personal survival. (Bob never pretended it was anything else.) But it was an example of straight thinking untrammeled by complicated sentiments.

In the wartime Army Air Forces, going over the head of one's superior is not quite as risky to one's career as it is in the peacetime Army or in General Motors. Of course, it could have been considerably more touchy to go over Carlson's head, and possibly fatal to bypass Colonel Mo. Even though he commanded *Tondelayo*, Johnny was, after all, a mere lieutenant. To question his wisdom or his competence was not regarded as *lèse majesté*. Moreover, *Tondelayo*'s abortions had become a minor scandal.

Years later when I talked with Colonel Mo he recollected the affair only dimly. He trotted out statistics showing that the 379th had the lowest abortion rate in the ETO. Statistics, however, are notoriously obliging witnesses. Whatever may have happened toward the end of the war to redress the balance, in those summer months of 1943 abortions were a serious problem, Colonel Mo admits.

"I got rid of him fast, didn't I?" the colonel asks.

In a way he did. Johnny was transferred to another crew as a co-pilot. He said nothing when he moved out of the hut. He packed his things. He grinned. There was nothing more—or nothing that anyone's memory can give back to us.

He may have stormed and shaken his fist. Perhaps he shook hands with each of us. He may have smashed the furniture or spat. There is a blank in my mind and in my notes and in those of my crew whom I can still find. There is only the memory of a grin.

8

Bohn slipped into the pilot's seat with a minimum of celebration. I was pleased. Bohn had a reassuring array of virtues concerning which he was properly discreet. He never made an offensive display of them, though I think that rumors spread of his excessive sobriety and these probably slowed his advancement. In Duffy's Tavern or in the pubs of town Bohn would step outside to look at the evening sky before taking so much as a half pint of bitter. If he could see stars he would back away from the bar, smile and go home to await a possible alert. He never looked down his nose at those who drank, but even I, who was no hell-raiser, felt a silent reproach at the sight of my pilot freshly bathed, his hair combed and gleaming, propped in his bed and reading when I came in late and noisy. He never mentioned the matter, of course. A church spire pointing heavenward carries a wordless message.

His language was tidy in a setting in which the

conventions called for a gaudier choice of words, sometimes imaginative, often resorting to the mechanical
interposition of "fuck" between syllables as in "Louisi-
fuckin'-ana." (This Americanism was merely updating
Joseph Pulitzer, who once told an editor he was too
"inde-goddamned-pendent.") Bohn heard it all and never
frowned. For emphasis he would occasionally give way to
"hell" or "damn." Pulitzer's "goddamn" would be too
offensive. I think Bohn was religious, but his faith was a
private matter and I did not intrude.

He had a pleasant, ironic sense of humor and a
realization of responsibility that was almost compulsive.
He knew what it was to fly; he was not merely pushing
an enormous collection of metal parts about the sky. He
was a part of the plane as the brain is part of the body, as
the spirit is part of the whole. He felt the glory of flight
although he corked such lyrical emotions as did we all
according to the cliché we lived by. We lived in front of a
mirror and hoped to die that way seeing at least our own
approval in the glass.

The rest of the crew was relieved at Bohn's accession.
Some may have felt a trifle uneasy because he did not fit
the specifications of the model fly-boy. The colonel would
not lavish any favor on him which might furnish crumbs
of advantage to us. (Actually, some decades after the war
when I saw Colonel Mo it was no surprise that he had
forgotten Bohn and me and *Tondelayo*. He did remember
Mike, our tail gunner, partly for his brilliant gunnery
record in downed Germans and partly for a certain
flamboyance which Mike knew how to mix with seeming
deference.)

Mike remembers that Bohn carried a checkbook in
those days, which impressed us all. He could bail out
members of the crew with a timely draft on a Minnesota

bank. "Of course we liked him. He was our banker," says Mike. "You got to trust a banker. He could have owned the fuckin' airplane."

For two hours or so on a cloudy July afternoon we cruised over the Midlands with our new pilot while the squadron operations officer checked him out as we would check out a new engine. Bohn passed inspection, but the operations officer had yet to check him in combat.

On Bastille Day *Tondelayo*'s crew was stood down, but I was assigned to fly to Paris with another crew. I felt uneasy, as if I were going alone to a party full of strangers. We hit Villacoublay, a fighter field outside the city. Paris was below my starboard window, blue-gray and smoky, with the Seine meandering through it. The French underground had sent word asking that we try to schedule our visits to Paris on holidays when few Frenchmen would be at work. A year earlier, after three hundred civilians had died in an American raid, Parisians thought the price too high for a very brief delay in German military production.

The flak had been heavier that day than expected, but we made it back with only a few minor scars on the plane whose name I no longer recall. I told Bohn that I could see the Champs-Élysées, and he smiled at what he called my tourism.

After that came days of false starts. We set out for Hanover, but halfway into Holland, facing a wall of cumulus cloud, we got the call to turn back. We went off to Hamburg but somehow failed to rendezvous with the other groups on the mission. Rather than feed our little band of twenty-four planes to the rapacious Luftwaffe, we went home. Bohn had to wait for his taste of combat as commander.

One morning we went off to Kassel, deep inside

Germany. The operations officer took his place in the co-pilot's seat. Again clouds lay below us like a protective shield over Germany. Knowing that the target would be covered, we headed up along the coast and dropped our bombs over what we thought was Kiel. I do not know what destruction we wrought that day, but we won the approval of our operations officer. He thought Bohn cool under fire, which was considerably more than Bohn had to say for him. The operations officer had been shaken by the spectacle of German fighters rising in swarms through the undercast.

Certainly he seemed a bit unstrung after we landed and took the usual survey of *Tondelayo*. The 20.-mm holes in two propeller blades caused the ground crew to gape in wonderment. Why those props should have continued to turn was a mystery. In high excitement Bohn took snapshots of the blades. Even more sobering, however, was that day's tally: of seventy-six planes that went over the target, twenty-two did not return.

The following morning we were up again in the cold predawn to find ourselves a broken family. *Tondelayo* was being fitted with new props. The colonel had commandeered our gunners for his lead ship—a tribute, of course. Bohn was to replace Mike in the tail position, as was the custom when the colonel took over. And since Dutch, the group navigator, would be riding with the colonel, I was fobbed off on a squadron lead.

Johnny was assigned as co-pilot with still another crew. We had been operational for almost two months and we had lost seventy-five percent of our original crews. Replacements were arriving, but as Arnold reminded Eaker, we had to salvage what we could. To some Johnny must have looked salvageable.

We do not know precisely what went on inside the

cockpit of Johnny's plane on the mission that day. Some said they saw the plane slip back and drop below the formation with one engine smoking, then blazing. Four chutes opened, they say. I was not there, because the plane on which I rode that day developed one of those mechanical symptoms that used to afflict us in Johnny's time. Again the cockpit asked me for a heading home, and after five hours we made it back to Kimbolton for coffee and the anxious tally of our wild geese. They came in across a sweep of sky still brilliant in the late afternoon.

I look over my time sheet that has been so scrupulously kept by some company clerk, and I am incredulous. One day follows another in the list of battles. There should have been time to savor and digest our fears. If on a Wednesday one watches other men die and sees one's own death foreshadowed, it does not seem fitting to watch a similar deadly dance on Thursday and again on Friday and again on Saturday. Such a schedule can make the most awesome event a dull routine and turn battle into a business. If some morning at my present age I saw my friend and neighbor killed or if I felt the whoosh of a bullet pass my head I should want some time to think and then to scream before I faced a similar ordeal. But in those days we were too young to scream and thoughts were easily put off by the exhilaration of death's presence. Now I can see that death is pallid and often ugly, but I confess it did not seem so then. And so we went up morning after morning in that gentle July, and on the thirtieth of that month we came to a strange milestone on the road to Schweinfurt.

It was a return visit to Kassel. We had been in action for four days running. At 0530 we were gathered in the briefing room, its bustle and its tensions as homey as a country kitchen, so quickly does the shocking become familiar. I do not remember fatigue. I had slept soundly and waked to the usual electric glare. I had bolted the usual eggs which seemed to coat one's teeth and tongue with fine sandpaper. I had scalded my throat with coffee and smiled at myself picking a poppy. Between a yawn and a sneeze I read our fate in chalk on the battle lineup.

I do not mean to say it was a routine like a ride in the subway betwixt sleep and waking, staring at faces and behinds that are different and yet the same day after day. It would distort the reality and stretch words out of joint to pretend that it could have been so dull. In a subway the imminence of death is conjectural, problematic. In the briefing room it was certain, fierce, palpable and stimulating.

We ten in *Tondelayo* circled over Yorkshire, warming ourselves in the sun at eleven thousand feet, above a gray expanse of cloud. We crossed Felixstowe heading southeast at 0730, according to the map that has grown old with me for thirty-five years.

We climbed to our bombing altitude, 24,000 feet, over the North Sea and hit the Belgian coast close to the Dutch border. Out the port-side window I could see the Scheldt winding into Holland, and out the starboard window lay Bruges. It was then that our own P-47s and the RAF Bostons waggled their wings and went home. It was 0801, I noted in my log. A scribble nearby I take to mean that there were fighters. They had swarmed up from Woensdrecht Airdrome. Actually some B-26s had preceded us in the hope of drawing them off. I do not know whether those bright-yellow-nosed spitting wonders had risen to the bait of the B-26s and then gone down to gas up in time for us. Perhaps they had wisely

Tondelayo and the author, 1943.

Bohn Fawkes, pilot—a cool man, exquisitely fastidious in matters of principle.

Bob Hejny, bombardier—a joyful man who could also seethe with rage.

The Kugelfischer ball-bearing plant at Schweinfurt on the Regnitz River as it looked when the attack began and later *(below)* after succeeding waves of bombers had obscured it with vast clouds of fire and smoke.

En route to Stuttgart, September 6, 1943, only hours before *Tondelayo* plunged to the bottom of the English Channel.

Flying Fortresses fall in various ways. A Messerschmitt's cannon has sliced a wing from this B-17.

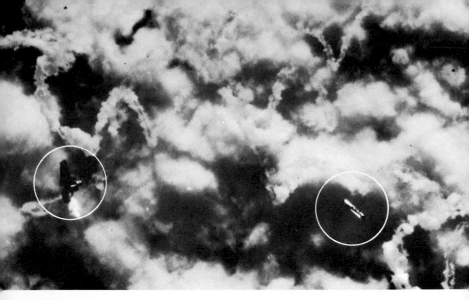

Above: the fuselage of this stricken Fortress has separated and each part *(marked by white ring)* whirls its own mad way about the sky leaving contorted spirals of smoke and flame. *Below:* sometimes the nose, and cockpit vanish along with pilot, co-pilot, engineer, bombardier and navigator. Here a B-17 over the target falls to earth along with the bombs from its sister ships.

Fire and smoke engulf the tail of a plane that continues to fly. A moment longer on the straight-and-level and some of the crew may get out.

At Kassel the flak rocks us and peppers us with shrapnel.

Vapor trails lend an ironically esthetic touch to combat. When the early morning sun catches us as we leave England, even our deadly machinery acquires a stirring beauty.

The low squadron superimposes its pattern on that made by tilled fields and canals.

Above us over the target roars a Fortress of the high squadron with bomb-bay doors open.

Colonel Mo Preston in a solemn ceremonial moment as General Robert B. Williams arrives to hand out decorations, mainly for the difficult feat of survival.

sent up only a few to greet our decoys and held the rest in reserve for the main show.

In any case there they were, buzzing up at us from an airfield right on course. This was ideal for the Luftwaffe, because almost all of the fighters' flying time could be spent in combat. In the previous April the Luftwaffe had fitted auxiliary fuel tanks to its fighters, which gave them perhaps two hours of high-speed, high-altitude flying time. On the day we went to Kassel the German dispatchers displayed their ingenuity by having their fighter squadrons hedge-hop from station to station along our presumed course.

Some came from Lille and arrived in time to give us trouble east of Brussels at 0817. Others came up from an airfield near Poix, too late to catch us on the way in but in plenty of time to ambush us on the way out. Some came from Brittany and Normandy and refueled at Lille.

At 0836 we were south of the Ruhr. We had weathered three heavy fighter attacks. Most of them came in from the rear of the formation, often four abreast. We in the nose felt their presence and heard the *ping* of shrapnel, but it was Mike who saw most of the action on the way in. Being a tail gunner is a lonely job. "It's a good spot for praying," Mike had said once. "You're on your knees all the time." The only spot that's worse is the ball turret, where the gunner is wrapped around his gun like an anchovy or a fetus in a womb too small.

The tail usually saw more action than the belly. "The fuckin' Germans must think all tail gunners are stupid," Mike used to say. They came in again and again, firing, turning bottoms up and slipping away.

From Gladbeck and Cologne swarms of FW's and ME's shot up and barreled through our formation. Near

Remagen I noted the fall of two enemy fighters. I fired at those arrows in the sky, but I knew that I was merely making noise to let them know we were alive on the port side. Bob's gun kept up a ceaseless chatter and the top turret pounded like a jackhammer inside my head. Then quite suddenly the fighters vanished and left us to our bomb run and the accompanying flak. We came up on Kassel from the south. I peered over Bob's shoulder and saw the city. We were rocked by flak. Still the motors ground on. There could be no evasive action. We would fly unswervingly through a sky of angry black shell bursts.

The bomb-bay doors of the plane ahead of us swung open. I watched the bombs tumble out helter-skelter at first, then straightening to a purposive plunge. When ours were gone, lost in the black smoke far below, Bob called out that the doors were closed and Bohn banked *Tondelayo* sharply to starboard. As we headed north and then west for home the flak slackened off and the fighters came back. They had been gathering all morning. It had been one hour and eleven minutes since we had entered Europe, and the Germans had had time to assemble a massive fleet of fighters, gassed up and ready.

It must have been somewhere near Recklinghausen that disaster struck. Mike called in to say he was hit in his right hand and left leg. Then followed a jumble of static and for a while we couldn't raise him at all. *Tondelayo* was being knocked about the sky. Actually Bohn was climbing, diving and making corkscrew patterns in a crazy choreography designed to unsettle the fighters, who were pressing in from all sides. I kept my mind on the zigzag line we were taking across Europe. When I tried to stand, my feet slipped from under me. I clung to my desk and the gun, waiting for the attack to subside. When at last Mike came on again his words were jumbled and he sounded as if he were calling from a painfully long distance.

We drove across Germany trying to keep up with the formation, which had a ragged look, with gaping holes where planes had been. I had seen two of the group go down. The formation was turning more to the south in a beeline out of Germany, when we became aware of an alteration in the sound of flight. When Larry in the top turret eased up and when Bob's guns stopped momentarily, *Tondelayo* seemed unnaturally quiet. The roar from the waist was missing. No one sang out to claim a kill or warn of fighters coming in. Bob and I looked at each other across the tops of our masks and he opened up his mike, ripping into my headset, "Bombardier to waist gunners, bombardier to waist gunners. Come in, come in." Silence. *Tondelayo* climbed and plunged. "Stockman, Herrin, come in, Goddammit. Come in. Do you read me? Duke, come in. Bombardier to radio. Duke, come in."

Tondelayo's motors whined. Then came Mike's voice, vague, blurred, with an odd calm: "They're gone. Gone."

We were 25,000 feet above Germany and they were gone. One imagines a switchboard operator saying, "Sorry, sir. They're gone." At the time the word itself with its nonsensical associations filled my head and left no room for irony. They had gone four miles down to the patchwork of farms I could barely see. Fighters were swarming about us, coming in at three, four, seven and eight o'clock where our guns were silent. Now and then we thought we heard a long burst from the tail, but that was all.

Bob disentangled his headset and oxygen hose. He lurched past me. His face was neither sad nor scared. I

realized that he was in a rage. He went up the stepway
to the cockpit. We were still in formation. I put down my
pencil, unplugged my oxygen hose and my headset. I
chucked my helmet aside and clambered after him.
Behind the cockpit Bohn pointed to a green oxygen
bottle, into which I plugged my hose like the antenna of
an insect. We ducked under the turret, which was
rattling in uninterrupted air-shattering streams of fire
that had the sound of panic. We passed through the
bomb bay along the narrow steel catwalk, past the racks
that had held the bombs, and into the radio compartment. Duke was gone. We went into the waist, where
blasts of cold air bit into my face. Herrin and Stockman
were gone. Their masks, still attached to the oxygen
outlet, flapped against the metal wall. The door had been
jettisoned. Through it we stared at windy space. As
Tondelayo banked and rolled I could see the distant,
detached world below. Then I saw Duke. He was sitting
on the floor, one leg dangling beyond the open hatch. Bob
and I pulled him in across the floor past the waist ports,
where the wind howled as in an arctic blizzard, where
one could see the silvery wings of our enemies curvetting
and spitting sparks.

The floor of the fuselage was torn in spots, the metal
peeled back. Multicolored cables were in shreds. We sat
Duke up in the radio room and looked to see whether he
was bleeding. He was untouched, but his eyes were
dreamy and he wore a smile of absurd serenity.

There was no oxygen in the rear of the plane. Mike
had seen the waist gunners as they jumped, driven by
lack of oxygen to illusions of impending disaster. Mike
had watched their chutes open. One of them had barely
cleared the horizontal stabilizer. Mike himself did not
know whether the plane was actually going down. In

any case there was nothing he could do about it. His arm and leg were torn and, though he was not in pain, he was groggy. He must have felt the cold, because the wires that hooked his electric suit had been cut. With his good arm he had changed the belt of ammo in his gun and eased his nerves by firing. He recalls seeing a Messerschmitt. He waited until it was two hundred yards from us, just the point, he thought, where the German would open up and blast us out of the sky. Mike let go a stream of fire that caught the fighter. It turned yellow and red, nosed upward, then spun in.

Bob hooked Duke to an oxygen bottle and stayed to take care of Mike as best he could. I hurried down to the nose, told Bohn the situation and began to work out a heading home. We had to drop to an inhabitable altitude regardless of the dangers of straggling in enemy skies. I remember looking at my watch, the minute and second hands whirling as unconcernedly as if I were on a street corner waiting for Esther. I looked out the window and, without seeming to grasp the significance of the phenomenon, noted that the propeller on engine Number Four was rigidly stationary. It had been feathered, disconnected to keep it from tearing the engine out of the wing. Black smoke streamed behind it. I drew a course that would take us across Holland dodging the flak zones listed in my flight plans. I hoped the information was reliable. I did not know. I only pretended to know. The plane dropped closer to the land. When I identified the Willems Canal in Holland, I called the cockpit to correct our heading. Our formation was above and ahead. We were alone. Mike's gun rattled, but I did not know whether he was firing at something or to keep himself awake. The top turret answered with a roar. But then came the blessed moment when I could tear off my tin hat and my mask and breathe real air. The plexiglass of the nose had several gaping holes. We had one man wounded. We were missing two others. But we were going home. We were going to drink something hot. We were going to sleep in a bed.

The ball-turret gunner, undoubtedly anoxic as were the others in the rear of the plane, could not easily raise his turret to extricate himself without hydraulic pressure, and that had been lost when the lines were severed. Curled up in *Tondelayo*'s steel ball, impotent, Leary had survived because he could not follow the waist gunners out of the plane. He was barely nineteen years old, the youngest in the crew. I do not know how he withstood that torture wrapped within himself, powerless amid bullets and explosions, oppressed by the realization that at any instant he might be spattered to a mass of ugly tissue, like a cat run over on the highway. That might happen to any man in the crew, but the rest of us had the illusion of motion, of elbow room to give us security. There was nothing that Leary could do about his fate. He was as powerless as a rivet in his ball turret. He had been reduced to a neuter.

We could have brought up the ball turret by hand and released him, but we needed his gun as we needed Mike's. When we reached the North Sea and saw the gliding shapes of friendly P-47s we brought him up. I calculated an ETA and gave it to Bohn. His voice was as even as if we were sitting on our bunks. "Roger. Thank you, Benny."

With flares rising like Roman candles we came to Kimbolton. We bumped to a halt on the grass where we had come before when our brakes were undependable. We were late, but we were home. Mike was not badly hurt, according to our cheerful obstetrician.

136

"Our waist gunners are gone," we told the debriefing officer.

"Are what?"

"Are gone."

"What?"

"Gone."

This battle is distinguished by a postscript which was appended some thirty-five years after the event. Bohn and I were sitting on a porch in Tarrytown, New York, on a summer evening. We were rehashing the war as ex-warriors have done since civilization invented wars. We were not seeking to dress our memories in cinematic glories or dissolve them in an alcoholic haze as veterans do. We were seeking rather to collapse the wind out of nostalgia, to see the war plain. We were trying to mount our recollections on pins so that we could study them in various lights from various angles. We were seeking to approximate an objective account of what we had seen and done.

We were reconciling scrawls from our respective logs. For example, after a raid on Münster Bohn had written: "This will make a lot of Dutch Nazis." He no longer remembered what that meant. And I had scribbled on that day the one word "Eindhoven." I had forgotten why. We looked at a map and saw that Eindhoven was a Dutch town not far from the German border. At the ground speed of those antique planes we flew it would have been perhaps ten minutes from Münster.

Our memories fed each other. As we talked, the scrawls unlocked cobwebbed files in our minds until at last the two comments made sense. Münster had been cloud-covered, and our formation had turned away from the target. The bomb-bay doors of our group leader were open. So were ours. Suddenly the undercast rolled away, revealing a flat green and tawny countryside. I recognized the pattern of rivers and canals. When I saw the formation prepare to bomb I yelled into the intercom that we were over Holland. As I yelled the bombs fell, and I noted that we had hit Eindhoven. It was then that Bohn had summed up in his log the political consequences. (Incidentally, I have subsequently talked with several Dutchmen who graciously forgave us, but then, none of them was under our bombs at Eindhoven.)

In any case it was in this search of the past that we came to the Kassel raid and the disappearance of our waist gunners. Over Bohn's face came a characteristically odd, slightly mischievous grin. "You remember," said he, "that we were hit by twenty-millimeter shells."

That was not a singular experience for us, I pointed out. But these had hit our gas tanks, he recalled. That did indeed stir something in the archives of my brain. Somewhere I had even made a note of shell holes in gas tanks. I reflected on the miracle of a 20-mm. shell piercing the fuel tank without touching off an explosion.

Now Bohn licked his chops so that I could see that a revelation was on the verge. It was not the case of an unexploded shell in a gas tank, he said. It was not so simple a miracle. At the time Bohn too had thought it was no more than that. On the morning following Kassel, while I slept late and missed my breakfast, Bohn had gone down to ask our crew chief for that shell, as a souvenir of unbelievable luck. Marsden told Bohn that there had been not just one shell but eleven of them in the gas tanks—eleven unexploded shells where only one would have sufficed to blast us out of the sky with no time for chutes. It was as if the sea had been parted for us. Even after thirty-five years so awesome an event

138

leaves me shaken. But before Bohn finished the story there would be both more and less to wonder at. He spun it out.

Bohn was told that the shells had been sent to the armorers to be defused. The armorers told him that Intelligence had picked them up. They could not say why.

The professorial captain of intelligence confirmed the story. Eleven shells were in fact found in *Tondelayo's* tanks. No, he could not give one to Bohn. Sorry, he could not say why.

Eventually the captain broke down. Perhaps it was difficult to refuse a man like Bohn the evidence of a highly personal miracle. Perhaps it was because this captain of intelligence had briefed so many who had not come back that he treasured the one before him as a fragile relic. Or perhaps he told Bohn the truth because it was too delicious to keep to himself. He swore Bohn to secrecy.

The armorers who opened each of those shells had found no explosive charge. They were as clean as a whistle and as harmless. Empty? Not quite, said the captain, tantalizing Bohn as Bohn tantalized me.

One was not empty. It contained a carefully rolled piece of paper. On it was a scrawl in Czech. The intelligence captain had scoured Kimbolton for a man who could read Czech. The captain dropped his voice to a whisper before he repeated the message. Bohn imitated that whisper, and it set us to marveling as if the revelation were fresh and potent, not thirty-five years old and on its way to being a legend. Translated, the note read: "This is all we can do for you now."

9

At St. James's Palace a guard in battle dress emerged from his box, clattered, walloped and banged his rifle, flipped it here, flipped it there, stamped about and presented arms. I was the lone witness to the performance; he could have carried it out only in my honor. I was as embarrassed as if I had broken wind in Westminster Abbey. I saluted smilingly. Unsmiling, he reversed the process, unwinding himself rhythmically to his original position.

As clearly as I beheld that guard on solitary parade, I saw Charles I ride down Whitehall past the Admiralty building with its bare-branched forest of aerials to lay his head on a black-draped block. There were ducks and governesses and seedy men with stained mustaches sipping their morning tea in the park across the road from Charles's Scaffold.

A yellow August haze cloaks these recollections of London during the frantic twenty-four-hour passes which we snatched between battles. From the Victoria Embankment near the monument to abolitionists with its playful gimcrackery I watched the shaggy tugs, snorting like buffaloes. And I looked longingly at American tankers. On these vessels, available to airmen who could talk their way on board, were sumptuous steaks topped with eggs, such as were found nowhere else in England or in any army mess except the rear-echelon, top-Brass hostelries at Wing or SHAEF.

I watched Hogarth draw gin-soaked whores on Bethnal Green. I saw *Love for Love* with Pepys at the Haymarket, and called, "Author." Just off Berkeley Square, at No. 4 Charles Street, there stood a narrow gray stone house that is a delicious memory. Its architecture had the tired elegance and subdued good manners of its neighbors, many of which were boarded up, their owners gone to war or to the country. It had mullioned bay windows, a brass knocker and a cast-iron gate.

Inside, all pretensions were dropped. The carpeting was worn. The hat rack and umbrella stand, commonplace and rickety, no longer expected to be used. A man stepped out to take one's coat, but he was more host than doorman. He wore a light pullover, as I recall. Down the stairwell of an evening drifted a blend of beef stew, Bovril, tobacco, gin and the tinkling of a piano.

There was an undeniable touch of snobbery in the excessive casualness of the place, like a duchess in denim, but I do not think it spoiled the stew or flattened the whiskey. It was called—pointlessly, so far as I know—the Brevet Club, reserved for flyers only. Though restricted to airmen, it was open to all ranks of all countries. The membership fee was negligible. The privileges: admission to the bar and restaurant, where

142

despite your card you had to pay your way; and a bed in a dorm for three or four at a modest price, with tea brought up in the morning by the barmaid. Actually what the Brevet offered above all else was admission to a circle of warming reassurance, which is the *raison d'être* for all exclusive clubs.

I do not remember the piano player's name, but I recall the genial cascade of his music, his watery blue eyes, and his ironic grin. He was the husband of the barmaid, and if she thought he could handle another scotch she would let you set it up on the piano. He said his thanks with a grin and let his fingers dance an extra flourish on the keys in your honor. His playing was glib and tolerable for hours at a time under appropriate alcoholic anesthesia. The bar was crowded, usually with British, Australians, New Zealanders, Canadians, South Africans, Free French, Poles, Czechs and a handful of Americans. The talk tinkled like the piano.

Looking at the date, it is tempting to suppose that we celebrated the overthrow of Mussolini or some other cataclysmic event of the world outside. I do not recall the world breaking in upon us, but if we did discuss Mussolini's end I am sure it was as if the event took place in a movie or in a different, remote, perhaps fictional war. The Brevet was not made for Grand Guignol or for solemn politics. It was a place for lullabies, for seductions.

In the morning I had been over Germany watching *Tondelayo*'s sister plane through my port window. Along the fuselage to the tail ran a scarlet streak. It had taken me a moment to understand that there was no top turret and that the fuselage was painted with the blood of a gunner who had manned it before it was blown away. And here I was in the evening, charmed by total irrelevancies at the Brevet. I talked and smiled as if I had not seen what I had seen only some ten hours earlier.

It was hard to say which was reality and which was escape. I experienced battle in my innermost gut and in every threadlike nerve. I registered it in the secretions of my glands and in the convolutions of my brain. With death visible and audible, creating a taste in my mouth and a flatus in my belly, I was undeniably alive in battle. At the Brevet, on the other hand, we all might have been pleasantly dead. I can remember nothing we said and very little that we did. I sank willingly down into it, however, as to a sleep.

The Brevet was the other side of the war. It lapped me in feathers and love. Perhaps when people die at peace and without pain they hear the tinkling of a piano.

Most of the time I came alone to London. Bohn came down now and then to the Brevet. Once I brought Duke along, but he had no time to spare for the club. He had molded all the exigencies of war into a very satisfying arrangement. It was an affair but not a love affair— nothing so stormy and operatic as that. It was an arrangement devised by and for people who liked each other and would not press their luck beyond the confines of that relationship.

Duke's lady was married to a thriving and talented commercial artist. They lived in a pleasant cottage in Surrey. The lady liked but had long since ceased to love her husband, an evolution which, happily, both had undergone simultaneously. They could therefore live together, on occasion eat together, talk pleasantly to each other and go to the theater, but they had no interest in making love to each other. Along came Duke, a very likable Yank whose company pleased the wife in bed and delighted both wife and husband at breakfast. Duke, therefore, had little time for me or the Brevet on his infrequent passes.

Once I brought Joyce to London. Joyce was not an anodyne like the Brevet. She brought the war with her. She could not help but do so. Her scrapbook was an amulet against desire. I could not take it from her. I held her body in my arms and she hid her frightened face in my shoulder. Compassion and fright—both of which I suppose we shared—are not the most inspiring emotions in bed. We managed the steps of the dance as an obligation to the time and to each other, and then in relief we slept, happy in the knowledge that our duty had been done.

When we stood again in Joyce's parlor in Bedford with her ma and da beaming at us, we tried to make our faces lie so that the world might believe we had reveled in regulation wartime lechery. We looked at each other and laughed.

Our war did not allow for sustained emotions. It spattered the brain with images of headless corpses, then washed it clean with the sight of a girl laughing at the piano player, then shattered it again with a dying plane sending its sacrificial smoke into the sky. It froze the brain at twenty below, boiled it with the smell of gunpowder, and let it fall asleep in a pub. Then it shook the brain, laughed at it, needled it with insidious thoughts of Esther and the child she carried, seduced it with the magic of London and the sweet sounds of the faraway and undiscovered. The brain split apart with the explosion of an airplane on the ground and the ritual rifle volley over the grave of the dead. Then it wrapped itself in the flow of talk around the barracks stove, homey talk of English whores or cockteasers—depending

145

on whether the speaker had won or lost the endless chase.

This was not the war of boredom and vermin we had read about in the tales of our fathers' agony. This was a frenzy in which I heaved and sweated but could not stop because, shamefully, my guts loved what my head hated.

I wish I could say that I knew then that other Jews had fought in the Warsaw ghetto that bloody spring and summer and that I had watched their fight as I did my own. But I cannot say that much for myself. I became obsessed with my own war to the point where I could not grasp the war that other people fought—still less integrate all of our wars into a single cause. Perhaps it is necessary that those who fight a war be relieved of the distracting obligation to see its totality.

The lords of the war whose job it was to view that totality had set down in Casablanca their famous "directive," drafted in royal tones uncluttered by detail. The blanks had to be filled in by Eaker in High Wycombe. He in turn called in two brigadier generals—both high priests of strategic bombing who had been part of the Billy Mitchell tradition: Haywood S. Hansel, Jr., and Frederick L. Anderson. They, with the help of some British experts, put together a plan for combined bombing operations, thereafter to be enshrined as CBO.

They compiled an index purgatorius of some seventy targets in six industrial categories outlined by the COA. The difficulty in selecting targets lay in the lack of competent, detailed intelligence reports. American— and, to a much lesser degree, British—target selectors were guessing with minimal clues. Frequently they analyzed German industries by analogy with their American counterparts. If the destruction of an industry would be likely to have serious effects on production or morale in the United States it was assumed that Germany was similarly vulnerable. Differences in geography, industrial development, dispersion, fortification and logistics had to be ignored—a major weakness at a time when the merits of strategic bombing were about to be tested.

Inevitably there was waste on a grand scale such as only an American enterprise could afford. A petulant letter in the Air Forces archives illustrates the point. It is from a German refugee. Commenting on a news report of the destruction of a large cast-iron and steel mill in one of our raids, he points out somewhat testily that the particular plant had in fact been abandoned some thirteen years earlier and its machinery sold to various outfits scattered around Germany. He suggests that, rather than destroy empty shells of factories, the planners might profitably consult "persons who recently left those cities."

I doubt that General Eaker or the COA called in many refugees but they put together a package of strategic-bombing principles, fleshed out with whatever specifics they could cull from the work of the American COA and the newly formed British Ministry of Economic Warfare. In April, Eaker took the package to Washington for a formal presentation before the Joint Chiefs of Staff.

The Joint Chiefs were then gathering for a sequel to Casablanca. This was a conference code-named by anonymous scriptwriters "Trident." The meeting had been arranged because the American Navy under Admiral King was continuing to deflect Allied resources to the Pacific, thereby negating the great British victory in winning Roosevelt to a Hitler-first policy which would follow up North African successes with the long-awaited lunge at the Italian underbelly.

147

Elmer Bendiner

Churchill and his retinue were sailing to New York aboard the *Queen Mary,* which had been thoroughly fumigated to rid it of the bedbugs and the cockroaches that had proliferated while it was carrying GIs to Europe. Two days after the British party landed in New York and were whisked to Grand Central for their ride to Washington, the Allied victory in Tunis and Bizerte set church bells to pealing on both sides of the ocean. The Prime Minister and the President argued amicably over the war's priorities and perfunctorily approved the recommendations of the Joint Chiefs of Staff concerning the air offensive that was to bear the crisp label "Pointblank."

Issued on May 14, 1943, new directives outlined the air mission in terms which unleashed us not only to demolish military installations and war industries but also to sow terror among German civilians. In the language of the directives we were to "accomplish the progressive destruction and dislocation of the German military, industrial and economic system and the undermining of the morale of the German people to a point where their capacity for armed resistance is fatally weakened. This is construed as meaning so weakened as to permit initiation of final combined operations on the Continent."

Of course, the marching orders for Pointblank were not read to the troops. We did not need it. Despite Pointblank's explicit commitment to terror, our leaders expressed our regrets concerning the offensive we planned to commit. We clung to the semifiction that any bomb that fell upon civilians was an unfortunate lapse from technological perfection. Such lapses were a thousand times more unfortunate when our friends were victims, as happened in Antwerp, where a public square was mistaken for a military barracks. Eaker, who had formulated that splendid phrase about our unwillingness to throw the strategic bomber at the German man in the street, reluctantly recognized, as had his intellectual forebears Douhet and Mitchell, that terror is a part of war—certainly of a "people's war" in the twentieth century. We were responding to terror, and that fact made our mission more acceptable. The unromantic British had no trouble whatever in accepting it. Some German experts during and after the war did indeed object, but pious poses did not become them.

Pointblank called for the destruction not only of public morale but of submarine bases, construction plants, the aircraft industry, ball-bearing plants, oil installations, synthetic rubber factories and transport facilities. All had been on Colonel Perera's list. Among the specifics in Pointblank was an order for "a very deep penetration at Schweinfurt." (So far had things progressed since the offhand comment to Colonel Perera at the Swedish minister's house party when Schweinfurt was first dropped into the conversation like a gem of gossip.)

The directive continued: "This operation might be undertaken as a surprise attack in view of the tremendous advantages accrued from a successful destruction of these plants; however, it would be most unwise to attempt it until we are perfectly sure we have enough force to destroy the objective in a single operation. Any attempt to repeat such an attack will meet with very bitter opposition."

There is nothing in the record to show that our high command took particularly great pains to assure themselves of our ability to wipe out Schweinfurt in one blow. Actually there seemed no way in which such assurance could be had, given the level of intelligence gathering.

Ever since the war we have been served delightfully blood-tingling accounts of wartime espionage, of secret plots and counterplots to decode the enemy's communications or ingeniously dispose of enemy decoders. Yet none, so far as I know, has reported the gathering of such simple but crucial information as might be necessary for the success of a one-shot raid on Schweinfurt.

Nobody seems to have been assigned to give us an estimate of the vulnerability of the ball-bearing industry to a single decisive attack. No trench-coated agent reported on how soon German industry could rebuild such machinery. We did not know the solidity of the factory walls, the vulnerability of such machinery to incendiaries. We seemed to have known only one thing, that it would be costly in lives and planes. For that we needed no spies. In any case, Schweinfurt was put on the agenda as soon as Eaker got back from Washington with approval of the strategic-bombing offensive by the Joint Chiefs of Staff and by their chiefs. After that it was a matter of waiting for the proper weather and visibility over the doomed city.

A few crews were chosen to prepare, in some mysterious way, for the ordeal. We of *Tondelayo*'s crew were unaware of all this. We went on from day to day flying to battles which were not necessarily earmarked as historic but were nonetheless bloody. Beyond the work, there was mud and chatter, mail and diverting scandal.

For example, a tender-hearted Bedford girl had confided to a sergeant in her bed that the next day's target would be formidable and she hoped he'd catch a cold. She named the target, and when her information proved accurate that conscientious gunner, alarmed to think that the girls in town were being briefed before we were, took the matter up with S2. The girl freely admitted that she had had her information from a major who was given to making wholly unsolicited confidences in the aftermath of passion. The major was demoted and shipped back to the States—a kindly sentence for an infraction that might have led a couple of hundred men into the deadliest of ambushes. I do not know what happened to the conscientious sergeant or the compassionate girl. I would like to think that they were both decorated.

On rainy days when no passes were granted, time stretched us on the rack. Some drank, some played poker. Once Colonel Mo went to the control tower with a rifle while Rip Rohr, scouting for a target, seized a hapless bombardier's hat and tossed it in the air. Mo got it neatly.

Colonel Perera had returned to England in July. Reading the report of his committee one can picture the happy excitement of those merry analysts, sensing a posthumous victory for their patron saints. Perera wrote:

General Mitchell had argued for the supremacy of the air arm. General Douhet had claimed that mass attacks upon cities would bring a nation to its knees. The studies of the Air Corps Technical School had pointed the way to the selection of a limited number of individual targets as the key. Neither the Germans nor the British have been able to achieve the results envisioned by Douhet. Both lacked the types and numbers of aircraft necessary . . . no attempt had been made to pick out bottlenecks in the economy where destruction would have the most rapid and pervasive effects upon German powers of resistance. With the adoption of the combined Bomber Offensive, therefore, it could be said that a new era in warfare had commenced.

Such historical perspective is as essential to a strategist's view of battle as a pair of binoculars is to a balletomane in a balcony. For dancers onstage, however, or for soldiers in the field, binoculars and perspective are impermissible encumbrances. So we flew or cursed the mud or told bad jokes or wondered about children yet unborn or made love while the chessboard was being prepared for the Schweinfurt gambit.

10

In the early days of August 1943, the German government was presented with a report on the situation in Hamburg. That city had been hit night after night by the RAF and occasionally by Americans during the day. The effect was cumulative. The heat generated by incendiaries boiled the air upward, creating a semi-vacuum at ground level into which there rushed fiery hurricanes. The report describes the scene:

Trees three feet thick were broken off or were uprooted. Human beings were thrown to the ground or flung alive into the flames by winds which exceeded 150 miles an hour. The panic-stricken citizens knew not where to turn. Flames drove them from the shelter, but high-explosive bombs sent them scurrying back again. Once inside, they were suffocated by carbon-monoxide poisoning and their bodies reduced to ashes as though they had been placed in a crematorium, which is indeed what each shelter proved to be. The fortunate were those who

jumped into the canals and waterways and remained swimming or standing up to their necks in
water for hours until the heat should die down.

Many of the men who thus manipulated the primal
elements of fire, earth, air and water were mild and
tender fellows. I knew them well; I was one of them. We
were not unconcerned with the hell we left behind us.
The hells were perceived, however, only as pillars of
smoke, not as human anguish, and, happily for us,
soldiers inhibit their imaginations. Most of the flyers
who cracked up in combat did so out of fear for their own
lives, not out of remorse, which is a civilian luxury to be
enjoyed in peacetime. A German woman, Else Wendel,
who after the war set down her memoirs under the title
Hausfrau at War, recalled asking her husband which
side had started the aerial destruction of cities. Her
husband answered, "I'll tell you after the war. No one
knows the truth while it is going on."

It is possible that the survivors of Hamburg and other
devastated German cities considered all Allied flyers
monsters. If, decades after the war, one looks back at
Hamburg and Schweinfurt, a terrible equation threat-
ens to rise from the ruins. Were we and our enemies
really one and the same?

My own answer is an emphatic No. The equation is
false and a phantom. True, soldiers on all sides are much
alike, but Nazis cannot take cover in a soldier's uniform.
Hamburg and Schweinfurt may be equated with London
and Liverpool, but none of these with Dachau. Hitler
was not a military phenomenon.

It is smug to say that their cause was damned and ours
was blessed. Yet what other words will do to chop the
truth to digestible size? Thirty-five years after the event

that truth is still incontrovertible. I am willing to admit to the soldierly fraternity of well-intentioned killers all swastika-bearing Germans of my generation who were certifiably unable to hear what Hitler was saying or to read what he was writing or to feel the absence of their neighbors who had disappeared. I do not know where to find such living dead.

We, waiting to go to Schweinfurt, did not fully understand the torment of Hamburg, but if we had understood, would it have made a difference? Not likely. To some of us it would not have mattered as long as we trusted the tactical wisdom of our chiefs who said this was the way to end the war, to end the Nazis. Some of us would have thought it enough to know that this was the only way we could go home again. To others—but, I think, a very small minority—it would not have mattered because orders were orders. We were not an ideological army, if such an incongruity exists. Actually, those who spouted political convictions of any sort were suspect. But neither were we altogether mechanical in our loyalties. Most of us would have preferred a surgical technique by which we could excise the vital organs of Nazi Germany without unnecessary bloodshed. We clung to the theory that this was possible and that we were trying to accomplish it.

The area-bombing British and the pinpoint-bombing Americans had their headquarters conveniently close to each other near High Wycombe where in comfortable detachment from combat our commanders could consider such matters as the Hamburg fire storms and the impending test of strategic bombing at Schweinfurt. I never got to High Wycombe myself except to navigate some visiting Brass in and out, but friends have told me of the glories of the place, of silverware laid upon white

155

napery at mess, of flowers in vases, of white-jacketed orderlies. They confirmed the legend of semiprivate or even private rooms for mere lieutenants in a building that once housed a school for young ladies. There is the widely reported story of the buzzer placed at the side of each officer's bed with a sign beneath it sparking erotic fancies. Put there for the convenience of schoolgirls, not flyers, the sign read: "Ring for Mistress."

The working part of High Wycombe was not in the girls' school but in a building built into the side of a hill. It was there that the Schweinfurt mission took formal shape. Crews had been picked for special training at High Wycombe or at nearby bases. It is not clear to me or, apparently, to any other writer who has treated the preparations for Schweinfurt just what the Brass had in mind when they told a couple of hundred men in utmost confidence that they would soon be engaged on an extraordinary mission to a distant and fateful target, too secret to be identified even to those who were being briefed.

I had never understood how crews could prepare themselves for a mission to an unknown destination. True, they were shown photographs of factories, but not where they might be found. They were told only that the target would be far away, the opposition heavy. How can one prepare for that? Can a navigator calculate headings to an unknown city, past unknown flak concentrations, with or against unknown winds? Does a pilot prepare his mind for such a momentous flight differently than for less advertised battles? Do gunners sharpen their aim on anxiety fed by the unknown?

Obediently the crews showed up at the High Wycombe headquarters, dropped practice bombs in the waters around England and went home.

We who went on our daily routines of takeoffs into soup, of rallying in the blue and then either plunging into combat or chafing under the frustration of another scrub—we paid little mind to the rumors. I do not now recall whether any crew of the 379th was chosen for this leadership exercise. I assume there was one, isolated and detached from the life we led. If I thought about the matter at all I probably imagined that there was some new gadget being tested. We of *Tondelayo* had been involved in similar tryouts of Loran, a fascinating navigational game played with blips on a screen and with multicolored grids. We had also been chosen to test glide bombs over the North Sea. But in none of these experiments had secrecy been trumpeted so loudly.

Later, the expert disposition of the Luftwaffe's resources at the battle of Schweinfurt would cause some knowledgeable observers to wonder whether the Germans might have known the secret of High Wycombe before the combat flyers could guess it. I do not wish to treat the German intelligence agents as wizards and our own as chumps, but in those days, before the memoirs of the British cloak-and-dagger corps were written, we tended to be impressed by enemy displays of prowess. These were often spectacular, as when their English-language radio program broadcast a welcome to our group on its secret arrival in Kimbolton and went on to inform us—quite accurately, as it turned out—that the clock in our mess hall was precisely three minutes and twenty seconds fast. The skill of these spies may very well have been no more than the flashy talent of a card shark, but it did have an effect on our unsophisticated minds. We had no evidence at all of our own agents' abilities except in reports of weather over the target which were frequently wide of the mark. After all, we figured, if you can't spy effectively on the weather you're not likely to do too well with more obscure secrets.

The master planners may have imagined that they were tuning up selected crews as one tunes an engine. It seems from postwar accounts that some of these crews did their practicing at Bournemouth or at other play areas after they tired of hopping about England on pointless runs in preparation for they knew not what.

In High Wycombe's underground war room the mood was not playful. Choirboys are expected to be mischievous, but priests are not. When a general entered the precincts of the briefing room mere majors, captains and lieutenants flattened themselves against the nearest wall and sucked in their stomachs as if they were cadets in the presence of upperclassmen. Just such a ceremony took place on Monday, August 16, 1943. Bomber Command navigators, using the best available information from intelligence and from weathermen, had drawn the outlines of the mission others would fly. They had marked the times for turns, the ETA's for significant points of the journey, the enemy flak and fighter strength along each leg. All the data had been put upon a huge map on which red twine was strung from pin to pin.

The importance of the mission and the precedent-setting nature of the plan required the most solemn punctilio. Reports were delivered in staccato bursts by high-level bombardiers, navigators and pilots in impeccable uniform. There had been earlier briefings of the Brass for a Schweinfurt mission, but weather reports had always been disappointing. On August 16, there were no assurances of cloudless skies over Schweinfurt, but the prospects were distinctly brighter than they had been.

A rough scenario had been prepared in the headquarters of General Anderson and approved by General Eaker sometime in July. It was an ambitious scheme calling for the precise timing of a high-wire act. It involved 376 bombers and about 400 fighters, British and American. A force of 146 bombers under Colonel Curtis LeMay was to leave from Lowestoft, the easternmost point of England, zigzag over the North Sea to Holland, turn south into Belgium, southeast to Mannheim, Germany, then almost due east to Regensburg, just sixty miles from Nuremberg. There they were to drop their bombs on a Messerschmitt factory and head not back to England but southward over the Austrian Alps and northern Italy, across Sardinia and the Mediterranean to two desert bases on the Algerian–Tunisian border.

(Crews destined for the Regensburg–Africa run had their only advance inkling that this was to be an overnight excursion when they were advised to pack their toothbrushes.)

The Regensburg raid was to be a diversion, useful in itself if it slowed Messerschmitt production, but essentially designed to draw enemy fighters away from the big show at Schweinfurt, where we were to cut out the vital ball-bearing mechanism of Germany. The Regensburg group was also to test the feasibility of shuttle missions from England to Germany to Africa. Because the Regensburg raiders would be slowed by extra fuel tanks they would leave England nine minutes ahead of the main force. They would have to be well away from the Schweinfurt area and on to Regensburg before we arrived. It was vital to disperse the Luftwaffe as widely as possible.

The Schweinfurt attackers—230 Fortresses—were to

leave from farther south, crossing the coast at Orford-ness and Felixstowe, near The Naze, that estuary which runs inland to Ipswich. We were then to head directly down to those familiar Dutch islands, cross Belgium and enter Germany near Düren. We would turn at Würz-burg, and attack Schweinfurt from the south. Because the division bound for Regensburg would be leading the way into Europe it was expected to bear the brunt of the first attack. Most of the fighter escorts—some ninety-six Spits and an equal number of Thunderbolts—were as-signed to give them cover.

Medium bombers, mainly Mitchells and Typhoons, were to sweep the Pas de Calais as an added distraction. The orchestration was intricate, but at the briefing at High Wycombe on August 16 no one ventured even the mildest reservation. It was assumed that the performers were equal to the demands of the score.

The Brass in the briefing room nodded and rose. The lesser ranks stiffened to attention. The machinery was set in motion. Orders were relayed in the form of Telexes. First came the preliminary alerts on numbered field orders, then the field orders themselves, then other field orders superseding in whole or in part all previous orders. Telexes spelled out not only the targets and the numbers of crews required but the bomb loads, routes, assembly procedures, weather, timing, communications channels and call signs. Zero hour was set for 0830. At that moment all the planes were to be in the air in proper formation, ready to head for the targets along the prescribed courses.

All that night Telexes ground out late changes in the plan. "Stand by . . . stand by," the machines rattled and clicked between messages as if to avoid the tension of silence. It was in the evening that we at Kimbolton

entered the grand design to which so many had contrib-
uted from Billy Mitchell on. After supper we became
aware that we were to play a part, although we were not
given the script. I do not know that anyone actually told
us that something big was up. The Telex must have set
the air at Kimbolton to vibrating so that barmaids in the
pubs sensed it and the Woffords in Bedford stepped
outside to see if the sky promised a day for flying.

We had been to Le Bourget earlier that day and to
Amiens the day before. The mission that was now taking
shape would be our third in three days. Once again we
fell into bed and rose in the middle of the night. Once
again we stumbled through the dark and breakfasted on
ink-black tea. I had plucked my poppy from the field. We
had heard the Telexes rendered into plain airmen's
English, embellished by Rip Rohr's extraordinary explanation of the momentous nature of our mission. It was to
be up to us to end the bloody war that Tuesday morning,
we were told. We gathered under *Tondelayo's* wing and
waited.

We were to take off at 0540. A pale sun burned
through the mist at midmorning and warmed the hay-
field beyond the hardstand. We dared not leave the
plane. We dared not disconnect ourselves from the
current that kept our wires taut. A jeep came out with
tea and soggy sandwiches. Some of us were stretched out
with eyes half closed, simulating a sleep that would not
come.

Certainly we did not speak of Schweinfurt, war or
death. We might have talked about the colonel's cow
that chomped the grass outside his hut. Mo, whose
palate was offended by powdered milk, had bought the
cow from a Kimbolton farmer. To be sure that the cow
was absolutely free of disease he had had her examined

161

by a veterinarian who, by some military whimsy, had been assigned to the Eighth Air Force. Mo found a farm boy among the service personnel and assigned him to feed, milk and cherish the beast. Fresh, warm, unpasteurized milk with its pristine gamey odor was a luxury for front-line Brass but a scandal for lesser folk.

The cow story, even with our most imaginative embellishments, would have rattled dryly at such a time, but it was the sort of trivia on which our stability rested.

Mike's celebrated bed would have been a likelier theme. We would have teased him about it just enough to make him smile and tenderly call us bastards. One Sunday morning three weeks or so before Schweinfurt the adjutant on inspection came to Mike's barracks. He was a beefy, paddlefoot lieutenant who, it was said, deserved an embarrassment medal because he suffered so from the disorderly presence of combat soldiers. They upset his schedule and affronted his dignity. That Sunday morning he stopped in horror before Mike's bunk. The offending object had leaped to his eyes like an elephant in a dog show. He was aware of it from the moment he entered the barracks, but had taken his time, pausing before each bunk, running his finger over each footlocker, no doubt deliberating on the attitude he was to take at the impending confrontation.

Then he came to Mike's magnificent bed. It was a Hollywood bed—a wooden frame on which rested a box spring surmounted with a mattress that was gentle but firm. Alongside the humdrum GI cots it stood majestic as a fourposter.

The following Sunday the lieutenant was there again, and there was Mike and there was the Hollywood bed and the impasse. On the Sunday before Schweinfurt, Colonel Mo led the inspection party himself. Mike had vowed that he would not cave in. When first he saw the bed in the supply room he knew it was meant for a paddlefoot lieutenant. "My back is as good as an officer's," said Mike.

A court-martial had been threatened. Now Colonel Mo stood in front of Mike at the side of the Hollywood bed. The colonel towered over the little tail gunner, but gunners were in short supply. Mo looked at the bed and at the slight, ingratiating smile that flickered on Mike's face.

"I see you're sleeping well, Sergeant," said Colonel Mo, and he strode down the barracks aisle.

There on the hardstand we rehearsed yet again Mike's triumph. Again we told each other of how the shiteatingmotherfuckin' dogrobbers needed him to win the war. And we said "Amen," for Mike was shorthand for us all.

There was nothing more to say. We lay on the ground and scratched the bottom of our minds for trivia. Finding no tattered rag of conversation, we lay naked to our fears while the obscure sun climbed toward noon.

Earlier that morning at High Wycombe, Brigadier General Frederick L. Anderson was talking about the weather. The targets would be clear, the weathermen had said, but outside the windows of High Wycombe a cool wet blanket muffled the trees and rolled in the ditches at the side of the road. The word came in from base after base with the same discouraging news of a countryside under wraps.

The decision was up to Anderson, and he had to make it soon. Ordinarily, an attack could be postponed until afternoon, by which time the August sun might be expected to have burned off the ghastly vapors. But the Regensburg force could not be held for very long. An hour or two perhaps, but certainly no more, else the planes would never find their unfamiliar Algerian bases in the dark of evening. Reluctantly Anderson ordered the zero hour moved to 0930.

General Eaker watched the tops of trees materialize into view at his headquarters and thought that perhaps he was not the only airman in England to begin to see the sky. In any case the decision was not his; it was Bomber Command's; it was Anderson's. There is a comfort in realizing that the decision is for others to make.

Colonel Curtis LeMay's groups were stationed along the coast, and it was there that the fog lifted first as if some hand were tentatively folding back the blanket. On those fields, as soon as the ends of the runway could be seen from the tower the takeoff order was given though the ceiling was zero. LeMay and his division then circled over Norwich, waiting for the Schweinfurt group to spring up through the fleecy undercast to the south and west.

A fleet of fifty-four Spits and twelve fighter-bombers had shot out over the cloud-covered sea in the early dawn to draw the German fighters away to Brittany. They were called back before they reached the Continent, but by now the Luftwaffe's controllers in the Pas de Calais had been alerted as effectively as by a bugle call.

In any case so massive a fleet of planes over England could no more be hidden from the enemy's radar than could a herd of elephants slip unnoticed across an open savanna in broad daylight. At 0923 the German radar stations were watching the spectacle of LeMay's Fortresses plus eighty-seven Thunderbolts circling over The Wash.

With his own forces assembled in formation, LeMay waited for word from High Wycombe, where General Anderson wriggled on the hook of his responsibility, unsure of how to order history.

In a report to Eaker after the battle Anderson listed the factors that persuaded him to unleash his combat forces despite the fact that his battle plans were being shredded before his eyes. Weather forecasts indicated that Schweinfurt, so available, exposed and vulnerable this August 17, would shortly slip beneath an overcast and stay there for at least the next two weeks and maybe longer. Also, there was pressure from Washington, from Africa, from Russia to slow the German industrial machine. Moreover, Anderson felt a heavy responsibility to the ghost of Billy Mitchell. He was aware that the future of air power might well depend on victory or defeat at Schweinfurt. To scrub the first fully strategic air mission of the war would have been painful. To launch the mission, fouled as it already was, might prove disastrous. But could not the sun shining on Schweinfurt that August day miraculously cleanse the air and recoup the wavering fortunes of the air-power champions?

If, Anderson reasoned, the Schweinfurt forces could not follow the Regensburg assault by ten minutes as had been planned, perhaps a long delay, of three and a half hours, might be just as good. It would allow the pilots of the Spits and P-47s to come home, refuel, drink a cup of tea and be ready to ride escort over the Channel for the second time that day. And the Luftwaffe? With so long an intermission after the first act, might they not assume that the show was over? The fighters would be sent back to their home bases—to Münster, Jager, Schiphol—away from the route to Schweinfurt. With a little luck the Luftwaffe would be asleep when the Schweinfurt attackers swept over the European coast. It was an impromptu battle plan, but such have seemed brilliant when they turned out well, and no plan, however carefully plotted, is foolproof.

The countervailing thoughts of General Anderson that August are not available to us. Did he worry that he might not be accurately outguessing the Luftwaffe? Did he weigh the disadvantages of postponing Schweinfurt's doom against the value of a man's life, of ten men's lives, perhaps of twenty or thirty or forty or four hundred? How many lives was it worth to wipe out Schweinfurt that very day? How could he or anyone make such calculations? Undoubtedly he made them as generals and statesmen must—by a look at the sky, by a scratch of the head, by a consultation with his viscera and a glance at a mirror for an encouraging nod of approval.

LeMay crossed over Lowestoft at 0935. The Channel sparkled below him, for the cloud bank stopped at the edge of England. It continued to hover over the fields where other groups waited to take off for Schweinfurt. At 0952 the first contingents of Focke-Wulfs rose and circled over the European Channel coast in readiness. Farther inland other German fighter units were scrambling. At the hardstand at Kimbolton amid the swirling mist we waited, unaware that we were missing our cue.

Between 1030 and 1115 Spitfires and Typhoons swooped over Brittany. They had been scheduled to distract the enemy from the bombers, but they were too late to help LeMay's formations and hours too early to help us. At this stage the battle resembled a film that does not mesh with its sound track. Men fell before they were shot and lions roared while still asleep. We were out of synch.

The Fall of Fortresses

At 1030 General Anderson was again faced with the disagreeable necessity of coming to a decision. The mist was beginning to lift from the runways of the First Division where the Schweinfurt-bound crews were now in their sixth hour of anxious waiting, their spirits having gone soft and limp.

The General had to decide whether to send the mission to Schweinfurt even though most of his plans had already miscarried. The Regensburg decoys, the fighter escorts, the diversions and distractions so painstakingly plotted and timed in the scenario had fizzled. It must have been maddening to the high command to consider that this shambles had been caused by a climatic mischance that bottled England in mist while all of Germany lay open under smiling skies. As for us, we continued to wait impaled on our fears as in a nightmare.

The demands of economic warfare bade General Anderson to lift his hand and let us go. The stakes were vast. If German industry could be knocked out by the destruction of Schweinfurt the effects would be felt throughout the world and the glory of air power would be secure forever. Moreover, with the autumn fog waiting like a malevolent ghost, there was no telling when the ball-bearing factories of Kugelfischer, etc., would again be open to us.

Let them go, he decided. Appropriate Telexes went off to Brigadier General Robert Williams, who was to lead the Schweinfurt raid. He was a dapper one-eyed pilot who had been in the Air Corps when Billy Mitchell preached the gospel and the air war was the war of the future. He had flown in the prototypical Flying Fortresses on a Latin-American demonstration jaunt in the thirties.

167

At Kimbolton Colonel Mo got the message at 1040 and sped out in a jeep to his waiting plane. Green signal flares soared from the tower. I hoisted myself into the nose and tried to collect my scattered tools and disheveled spirit. I felt the coil springs tighten in my gut while a vague nausea stirred in my gorge. *Tondelayo* was an airless shell that had baked too long. The prop wash bent the tall grasses at the side of the hardstand as we taxied off.

Above The Wash and above the overcast I was at ease circling in the early-afternoon sun. I looked at the assembling formation and waited for the customary magic to do its work. As I think back on it I must have been addicted. Those dreamy circlings above the world seeped into my spirit like a narcotic, giving a cadence and a melody to the flow of my blood. Flabbiness and flatulence of earthbound limbo collapsed and dissolved. I was high; I was tight.

In flight we could tune our radios in to Germany, which interspersed its news programs with grandiloquent music. I would not append to these memoirs so obvious and mindless a sound track as "The Ride of the Valkyries," and yet it is that sort of music, hymning majestic passion, that I do recall hearing in my headset or perhaps rattling in my head.

Two hundred and thirty fortresses jockeyed for their assigned positions in the armada that was forming behind General Williams. We were flying in the lead of our wing. There were planes below us and above us, before us and behind us. A few of the 379th were flying off to our starboard and slightly above in a composite group. *Tondelayo* was right behind Colonel Mo's wing man, a comforting position.

At 1315 the entire formation was in place. Gleaning

in silver with white contrails spinning behind them, the Fortresses pulsed and throbbed. The sound of engines beat a rhythm for which my mind devised melodies. We strung out for perhaps ten miles or more across the sky as we left Orfordness.

I exulted in that parade. I confess this as an act of treason against the intellect, because I have seen dead men washed out of their turrets with a hose. But if one wants an intellectual view of war one must ask someone who has not seen it.

It was 1314 when we left the coast of England. We could see no vapor trails of friendly fighters as called for by the script. They may be up ahead, someone said, or far behind. There was nothing we could do about it and that was a comfort. No need to sweat. We left England at 15,000 feet and climbed to 24,000, a comfortable altitude for a B-17 but a difficult one for an ME-109 that gasps for air and uses its fuel fast at such a height like an old man puffing up the stairs. We wondered, therefore, when the wing ahead dropped to a lower altitude. We did not know why at the time, but Colonel Gross in the lead plane of that wing was impressed by a bank of clouds that seemed to wall off the Continent. He estimated that it would reach to 26,000 feet and that we might therefore be flying blind over a cloud-covered Europe despite the forecast. Better to stay under the overcast and find the road to Schweinfurt even if it meant flying at a height likely to be infested with Messerschmitts. It is a choice of the sort that colonels must make and with which others must live or die. Ten planes—one hundred men—went down from Colonel Gross's formation in the early stages of the battle. It was considered the colonel's error.

We stayed at our prescribed altitude, ascending through cloud and emerging still in formation radiant as

169

unbloodied lances with pennants flying. From my port-side window I could see no friendly plane. Out starboard, above the drift meter, the view was made more congenial by a Fortress, and up ahead there was Mo and his wing men.

I remember that while we were still over the Channel we spotted a B-17 far below us, heading for home. Actually eleven planes aborted before we reached the enemy coast. Any reason for an abort seems good enough at the time, whether it is prompted by engineering symptoms or more personal considerations. We felt no resentment, a bit of envy perhaps, countered by a feeling of tolerant superiority. It was understandable that some should leave, though in this case it meant that our invading force had lost the firepower of 121 machine guns. Fortunately such facts are computed after the event and do not affect the morale of those who are mercifully limited to their own tiny circle of war.

Over the Dutch islands I spotted fighters at eleven o'clock high. Their gray silhouettes slipped in and out of the frost patches on my window. Someone said they were Spits, and Bob turned back to wave cheerily at me as a sign of his immense relief. They paralleled our course. We were supposed to have Thunderbolts as well, but we saw none. (Actually they were nine minutes late in taking off and so missed us.) We were happy with the Spits, but we knew that this was only a matter of courtesy. We were being escorted to the door of Europe. It was a charming gesture, but we knew they would have to turn back. Within a few minutes we would have no difficulty in telling friend from foe, because there would be no friends.

The flak from the islands seemed inconsequential. A few bursts were at our altitude but very wide of the mark. The effort seemed pro forma, like a cuss word to show a proper hostility. I noted it in the log. It was at Antwerp that the first serious flak reached us. The Spits vanished at about that time. I did not see them waggle their wings in farewell, but I do not doubt they did as much, for they were mannerly as well as friendly.

Records of the battle, pieced together from Allied radio monitors and German postmortems, indicate that at 1351 two groups of Messerschmitts, already airborne, were ordered to intercept us east of Antwerp. They may have come from Schiphol or Oldenburg or perhaps Münster far to the east. They had not gone home to have their lunch and nap as General Anderson had hoped. They were up and waiting for us. Had they known we were coming? Had they guessed? They had landed at Woensdrecht earlier that morning while we were still circling over England, and they had been kept on alert for our arrival. Now they swarmed like gnats from the Belgian flatlands and the crisscross of canals.

We were somewhere between Antwerp and Aachen when I was aware of the first rocket attack. It seemed to come in from seven o'clock over *Tondelayo*'s left wing. I remember seeing a brownish object tumbling and then bursting into an orange-yellow flash and an enormous black cloud. *Tondelayo* reared like a frightened horse.

I do not recall seeing a rocket actually hit a B-17. I remember only the fireworks and the gust of wind. The smell and sight of battle are still with me—the acrid gunpowder and the disordered plexiglass cabin—but I cannot recall a sound of battle except the clump and clatter of our own guns. The throb of our engines was so monotonous as to leave an effect of profound quiet as if we were in a soundproof chamber beyond which the enemy whirled as in a silent cinema.

171

Elmer Bendiner

There was a running chronicle from the tail and the waist describing the fall of planes from the high group where six of the 379th had been assigned. "Plane in flames, chutes opening"; "Plane falling like a stone—no chutes." So it went. We droned on. When I was not at the gun I was scribbling in the log the time, place and altitude of flak, of rocket bursts, of kills and fallen comrades, of headings and checkpoints.

Can I have been so detached? Not to feel the heat of battle or the clutch of panic or the numbing chill of altitude? As a boy in a schoolyard could I have scribbled a note about my bloody nose and blackened eye? Could I have kept a pad by my bed to report the fierce and fond explosions of love? I doubt it. Yet I noted the events of battle like a metronome timing the music without hearing it. I do remember looking down somewhere after Eupen and counting the fitful yellow-orange flares I saw on the ground. At first—so dense am I—I did not understand them. Here were no cities burning. No haystack could make a fire visible in broad daylight 23,000 feet up. Then it came to me as it came to others— for I remember my headset crackling with the news— that these were B-17s blazing on the ground.

The afternoon was brilliant, but, as I remember it, the earth was somber, smudged, dark green and purple. In the gloom those orange-yellow fires curling black smoke upward were grotesque. I was as incredulous as I had been when first I saw a fuselage red with the blood of a gunner's head blasted along with his turret. As we followed that trail of torches it seemed unreal. I see it now as a funeral cortege with black-plumed horses and torches in the night.

Those who monitored German radio during the battle

heard the fighter pilots chatter. Clearly they underrated our strength and overrated theirs, but nonetheless their kill claims were far more accurate than ours. And they had the evidence of those blazing pyres to assure them of at least a partial victory at Schweinfurt.

From the initial point we could see a great pall of smoke hanging over Schweinfurt. There was no need for me to point out checkpoints along the Regnitz River, but I did.

There was no need for Bob to have studied the shape of the Kugelfischer Werke or the Vereingte Kugellager Fabriken or the building of Fichtel & Sachs. None of these were visible. All lay beneath black clouds and red flames. We saw Colonel Mo's doors swing open as he rode toward the column of smoke, terrible as a sign of judgment.

From Mo's plane tumbled sticks of bombs end over end and topsy-turvy like a child's toys falling off a table in slow motion. Slowly they righted themselves as if given a direction and meaning. Then, straight and regimented, the bombs fell away toward Schweinfurt. The flak was all about us, but the fighters were gone. We heard the *ping* of fragments rattling like pebbles against the flanks of *Tondelayo*. I noted the time as Bob cried out with an odd, cheery excitement, "Bombs away. Get the hell out of here."

Then we banked sharply and streaked away to the west and north. The flak was reported as intense and accurate over Schweinfurt, though neither Bohn nor I remember it as being more horrendous than at many other targets we had seen. We both recalled the deadly persistence of the fighters after the target. Again and again they came at us, through us, from dead ahead, from either side, usually from below but sometimes from above. They darted like dolphins amid a formation of plodding tugs.

In England monitors heard the German pilots gathering from all over France and Germany to ambush our homeward flight. German control was pinpointing our painful progress to Bonn, Aachen, Cambrai, Brussels.

All across Germany, Holland and Belgium the terrible landscape of burning planes unrolled beneath us. It seemed that we were littering Europe with our dead. We endured this awesome spectacle while we suffered a desperate chill. The cartridge casings were filling our nose compartment up to our ankles. My flak vest grew heavier as we proceeded until it seemed that I could survive everything but that weight of armor and the cold that twisted my guts.

At last we came to the blessed sight of soaring Thunderbolts above the Channel coast. It was 1659 by my watch. The afternoon sun warmed the port-side window. Then, with my armor off, I sat down and looked about me. I noted the altitude as we dropped, the look of the sea as we came nearer. I would have noted my heart's blood dripping to the floor—the time, place, altitude.

On the field at Kimbolton I counted the flak holes in *Tondelayo*. Then I felt exhaustion creeping in beneath the excitement like death beneath a fever.

We had been in the air for eight hours and forty minutes. We had been in incessant combat for close to six hours. It had been fourteen hours since we had risen in the predawn. In that time sixty B-17s had been shot down, six hundred men were missing. The first major strategic air battle of the war had been fought. Did we win? Did we lose? Did we really see those planes burning on the ground? Did we see this one fall and that one fart black smoke from his engine? Whose chute opened? Whose did not? Questions turned in the hollow mind bereft of thought, like an awl in wormwood, biting into nothingness, the nothingness of spent men at last asleep.

11

On the morning of August 18, 1943, while a mercifully soggy sky wrapped Kimbolton and let me sleep, the body of General Hans Jeschonnek, Chief of the General Staff of the German Air Force, was found in Berlin with a bullet through his head. A suicide note declared only that the General could not work with Goering and asked that the Reichsmarschall be banned from the funeral. I feel a modest responsibility for the General's death. I was at least a midge adding my weight to his last straw.

General Jeschonnek's prime function in the hierarchy had been to serve as a whipping boy on whom Hitler might exercise his histrionic rages whenever we or the RAF penetrated deeply into the Reich. The arrangement was most unfair to Jeschonnek; defensive strategy had never been his specialty or his concern. He had advocated terror à la Douhet, even as did "Bomber" Harris. He had pleaded with Hitler to let the Luftwaffe spread panic in the streets of British towns. The Führer had put him off with promises that such morale-destroying tactics would be used as a last resort. Now the German cities were under the terror and Jeschonnek had to bear the blame. He had taken a furious tongue-lashing only four days before Schweinfurt when we hit the aircraft plants at Wiener-Neustadt. He is quoted as having complained to his colleagues afterward, "Why does the Führer say all this to me and not to the Reichsmarschall?"

It is not known precisely what Hitler actually said to Jeschonnek after we left Schweinfurt, but it could not have been pleasant. And to make matters worse for the General, that very night the RAF attacked the Baltic island of Peenemünde, where in supposed secrecy the Germans were preparing rockets for the kind of anti-civilian terror that would have gladdened Jeschonnek's heart had he lived to see the V-2 blitz.

Acting perhaps on "disinformation" provided by the British, Jeschonnek had ordered a great many units of the Luftwaffe to rally over Berlin that night, and a German flak battery had shot down some of the misdirected planes. (Naïvely we had supposed that such monumental bungles were possible only in the anarchy of freedom. Had we known that despotism too could be so inefficient, we would have been mightily heartened.)

In any case it is not surprising that after so painful and humiliating a day and night General Jeschonnek should despair. His passing is only a footnote to the war, but it is a comfortable indication that for at least some hours on August 17 and 18 the Germans must have thought that it was we who had won the battle of Schweinfurt.

In the hours and days immediately after the battle our leaders felt so, too. While we were still over the Channel

General Anderson had announced that we had achieved our objectives at Schweinfurt. An industrious PR staff issued a release in the General's name, declaring triumphantly:

> Germany is now wide open—no part secure—for today she received two blows at vital units deeper in her territory than ever before. . . . the end of German power is but a matter of time. . . . although we cannot say that the end actually is in sight . . . the final effects of prolonged bombing of this kind are as inevitable as the chain of events necessary to build an enemy airplane. . . . we are breaking that chain in several places and many other chains along with it.

I don't recall that any of us read our notices on the day after our performance, but they were glowing. We had our "pincers" around Hitler's throat, it was reported. The early stories listed our losses as no more than two B-17s.

Our victory was officially termed a triumph for Billy Mitchell, for strategic bombing, and most particularly for the American Air Forces. General Hap Arnold in Washington gloated: "The American idea—high-altitude precision bombing—has come through a period of doubt and experimentation to triumphant vindication." Later, as reports trickled in to General Eaker's headquarters the triumph began to seem less brilliant, the vindication less certain.

In his report to Eaker, Anderson interpreted the reconaissance photos as cheerfully as possible. He called the Regensburg result "excellent," exulting in the fact that scarcely a building in the sprawling Messerschmitt factory there was undamaged. At Schweinfurt, on the other hand, bombing results could be described as

179

merely "good," he noted. Apparently we had scored direct hits on four machine shops of the Kugelfischer Werke, taken the roof off one machine shop of the Vereingte Kugellager Fabrik, damaged another and destroyed a pressing shop. We had burned out an office building, a canteen, a number of storage facilities and three unidentified structures within the factory complex.

We also damaged other enterprises that could scarcely be called strategic in the sense that the Reich would reel at their loss. For example, we gutted several sections of a fruit-preserving plant, crippled a malt factory, set on fire one wing of the Schweinfurt Town Hall, damaged a bank and put craters in two streets. We leveled two blocks of barracks and damaged seventeen others, knocked out a railroad station, one train, and a footbridge over the marshaling yards.

Although the results did not quite measure up to the promise of the Schweinfurt raid or to the premature announcement concerning the triumph of strategic bombing, unquestionably we had discommoded the enemy. Albert Speer, once Hitler's Minister of Armaments and War Production, whose memoirs are considered authoritative for all that they are self-serving, writes that Schweinfurt, which accounted for a little more than half of all Germany's ball bearings, suffered a thirty-four percent drop in production. In terms of the total national output of the vital little steel balls, the Reich was down some seventeen percent, a significant drop though not the fatal blow envisioned by the COA and by our commanders.

It is heartening to read that eight weeks after the raid, with reserves dwindling, workers were rushing the Schweinfurt output of ball bearings to factories in their knapsacks. The enemy's return to primitive transport is

one objective of strategic bombing which seeks to un-
ravel modern technology.

We of *Tondelayo* were quite unaware, of course, of how
well or how poorly we had done. For that matter, Bomber
Command, Eighth Air Force Headquarters, and even
Roosevelt and Churchill—then enjoying another rendezvous in Quebec—were all in the dark.

Eaker could not know whether Germany had been
given the hoped-for mortal blow by our strategic bombers, but he could and did make a precise count of our
losses: 60 planes, 552 men missing; 21 men brought back
wounded; 8 brought back dead; at least 17 of the
returned planes inoperable, many others heavily
damaged. He was in the position of a man who does not
know precisely what he has bought but is certain that it
was very expensive.

The battle was not only costly in men and in airplanes;
it might have meant the end of an idea that had brought
us from Billy Mitchell to Schweinfurt—the faith in
strategic bombing.

Within weeks Hap Arnold was in England appraising
the results for himself. Eaker hoped that such firsthand
observations of his shrunken resources would restrain
his chief from demanding, in streams of transoceanic
cables, just why massive formations of the Eighth Air
Force were not pounding the enemy day in and day out.
Arnold saw the need for long-range fighters to escort us
and promised to see that if any were delivered they
would not subsequently be diverted to Eisenhower in
North Africa.

It soon became clear that Schweinfurt had not been
put out of commission, but Arnold refrained from blam-
ing Eaker. "I'm sure you'll get it," he said, "as soon as
the weather permits." Though aware of our monumental

losses, Arnold continued to needle Eaker to have us up and at the enemy from dawn to dusk. There are generals who think it their duty to ceaselessly stir up subordinates with pep talks. A mere lieutenant would have cracked under such paternal needling; Eaker bore it as befits a general.

To complicate Eaker's life still more, there were problems on the ground of the sort that never troubled combat crews. Bombs and ammunition had to be hauled from depots to combat fields through mud and fog by soldiers who were frequently denied the right to sleep in barracks or eat in mess halls. At night they curled up in their trucks; they lived on K rations. They were all-black outfits at a time when only the starry-eyed could envision the integration of American mess halls without a bloody civil war. They were officered by whites who did nothing to prevent the "disturbances" that broke out that summer. Eaker found the whites responsible for ninety percent of the trouble and used his authority to curb at least the most blatant bigotry before it became a scandal and a damaging obstruction to the flow of vital material.

In the air or on the ground the summer of 1943 was an uneasy time, and Schweinfurt, despite euphoric public statements and exuberant journalism, did nothing to stir the spirit. Brigadier General Robert Williams, who led our wing at Schweinfurt, noted the universal unhappiness in a formal report.

He thought the bombing result disappointing; he was very unhappy about the failure of the P-47s to make the rendezvous with our bombers at the appointed hour, a lapse to which he attributed the loss of fifteen planes and crews, shot down along a stretch of the course that should have been under the protection of the Thunderbolts.

Williams reported "a sag in combat crew morale." He cited not only the loss of six hundred American flyers on August 17 but additional losses suffered by the RAF that night over Peenemünde. And what were they doing over Peenemünde, he wanted to know, when the Americans had the right to expect a follow-up attack to finish the job at Schweinfurt? At least four groups had been "decimated" by the raid, Williams said. He was not hopeful about mounting another offensive without replacements. Moreover, after so bloody a day, he reported, the men had expected a respite and instead were put on a continuous alert in the mud and drear of their bases.

In searching my memory for a substantiation of General Williams's report of widespread battle fatigue, I am driven to the conclusion that generals do not necessarily share the same war with lieutenants and sergeants. To expect otherwise, I suppose, is to imagine that horse and rider experience the same sensations during the gallop. I think that is a delusion of the rider.

The General felt that the first battle of Schweinfurt was the most horrendous engagement ever fought in the air. And so it was if one goes by the statistics. An ordinary soldier, however, judges whether an engagement has been tough by the effects on himself and on the men he knows. He fights in a narrow space barely big enough for his own terrors and triumphs. That other larger battle of gains and losses, victories and defeats, is something he reads about. For us on *Tondelayo* there had been other battles far more devastating than Schweinfurt. After all, we did not have to come home alone, and all four of our props were spinning when we landed. Our oxygen lines had allowed us to breathe. We had been hit, but in no vital spot, and all ten of us were alive, and unhurt.

Of course, we had followed the terrible trail of burning Fortresses, but the death of hundreds far away is not nearly so horrible as the death of one man next to you. Were it otherwise, no man could live out a single day of war, perhaps not even of peace.

For example, we followed the Schweinfurt raid with a few milk runs to France. It pleased our chiefs and the American public to know that we were working. These French excursions also perplexed the enemy, who, from all postwar accounts, could not understand why we did not continue to pound the ball-bearing plants while we had production schedules at least momentarily off balance. Actually, milk-run missions were the only ones we could have handled in our diminished state.

On August 24, the Eighth Air Force mustered 166 planes to hit targets in northern France, and only five were lost—a milk run for 161 crews and a mortal struggle for five. Then, on the twenty-seventh, 187 crews went to Watten. This was to be short and painless. The arrangements were very civilized: no call in the dead of night, no breakfast in the gray dawn. Briefings were set for 1000, and the predictions by our cheerful intelligence officer made it sound like an excursion to a public park.

Watten lies just over the Channel. We were not quite sure what was there, but we were to hit it anyway. The French had sent word that the Germans had just completed some major construction there and had laid off the work force. The secrecy around the project had tantalized Allied intelligence. Agents, picking up leads in Madrid cafés, had reported a series of stone platforms at a number of sites along the French coast including

Watten. Each one, measuring about 220 yards, was built on a hill facing England. (It was later discovered that these were to be the launching pads for V-2 rocket bombs that subsequently blitzed London.)

Neither the agents nor the intelligence chiefs in London had any notion that those cement pads would be absolutely impervious to our bombs.

We were to take off at two in the afternoon, fly at a comfortable altitude of fifteen thousand to eighteen thousand feet. (We could almost do it without oxygen.) We would be home by five. What was more delightful, we were to be well covered by Spits and Thunderbolts all the way in and all the way out.

We made it to the target all right and the weather was marvelous. Watten looked pretty even amid the light flak. Bob was convinced that our bombs were right on target. So were we all. Enemy fighters were sighted far off beyond our escort, and we watched a few indecisive dogfights in the distance as if we were aloof spectators.

Then out of the glaring sun, two—perhaps three—German fighters came blazing at us. It was as if we were the only plane in the sky and they were drawn to us as to a natural prey. I grabbed my gun, but I knew I was too late. I saw Bob working at his gun and I was shattered by the intolerably long, head-jarring roar of the top turret. It roared long after the fighters had vanished behind us, for Larry, our engineer, had frozen on his trigger and could not stop though he was shooting at an empty sky.

Fires were blazing out of our two inboard engines. Yellow flames whipped back along the fuselage. The plane pitched forward and I slid to the floor. I cannot say how one knows when a plane is deliberately put into a dive and is not plunging out of control, but the recognition is instantaneous. Actually Bohn was diving to stir a wind that might put out the oil fires. As we dived our wing men on both sides started down with us to cover us from attack. Then I saw them turn away. I did not understand that Bohn had waved them off for fear that if we exploded we might take them with us.

We dived until the oil fire went out on Number Three. Bohn killed Number Two engine and feathered the prop. Then we were alone in the sky with only our two outboard engines to take us home. I worked out a heading and we limped low over the sparkling sea into the sun. We could see the formation high above us en route to England. A few minutes earlier we had been with them on the milk run.

We came to Kimbolton firing distress flares into the crystalline sky of a fine summer afternoon. When we pulled over onto the grass, the ambulance and the fire engines were there. We sat for a while. We were no longer expected in the debriefing room or in the barracks. Crewmen of other planes had already reported us as going down in flames. We made it back to the hut anxious to be there before our bedding was rolled up, before our personal effects were packed and sealed, ready for our next of kin.

I was glad we forestalled that painful rite. Not only did I want the comfort of my home preserved intact, but Esther was waiting in a Brooklyn apartment for our child and I hoped to have a telegram at any hour of any day. I thought it would be nice to be where I could still be reached, and it would have been dreadful if Esther and not I had received a telegram.

12

For two weeks after Schweinfurt the Eighth Air Force dared not venture beyond the sheltering umbrella of P-47s and Spits. It was a time for "simpler tasks," as military historians have come to label our attacks on Watten, Villacoublay and Amiens, missions deadly only to those who died.

By September 6, however, Generals Eaker and Anderson felt that the transfusion of fresh men and planes had restored us to a condition of health in which we could again carry the flag deep into Germany. It is said that we could not afford another Schweinfurt just then. But if so, why did we go to Stuttgart, where the risks were almost as great and the promise of victory not nearly as meaningful? The distance was actually greater than to Schweinfurt and almost all of it over heavily defended parts of Germany. As a target Stuttgart offered some aircraft factories and some ball-bearing plants, but these were not nearly as important as those in Schweinfurt.

Evidence indicates that the trip was decidedly more important than its destination. We were to show our friends and enemies that two weeks after suffering a devastating loss of six hundred men and sixty planes we had the replacements, the spirit and the sense of theater to leap through other hoops of fire.

Part of the charm of the air war lay in its circus atmosphere. On some occasions we swung from a flying trapeze not to get to the other side of the tent but to win applause or tears, depending on the finale.

The circus aspect of the war was a symptom of our innocence. We believed in the political importance of brave gestures. We were appallingly juvenile. We beheld, without understanding, the premonitory signs of the breaking up of our age. We had only the merest inkling of the horrors of Hitler's Europe. The average civilian victims of those days, bearing their numbers tattooed on their flesh, knew far more of our terrifying century than did we who could shed our uniforms at the war's end. And as for the horrors that were still to come and were even then casting discernible shadows, we laughed at them. Some of us had the embarrassing misfortune to have laughed in print.

For example, on August 20, 1943, some two years before Hiroshima, while we were between Schweinfurt and Stuttgart, our daily paper, *Stars and Stripes,* brought us a tiny boxed item on page one. It was a United Press dispatch datelined Stockholm. This is the full text complete with head:

WHEW! HITLER HAS BOMB
SO POTENT HE'S SCARED
The secret weapon stories reached their ultimate today. The Germans here reported that Germany

188

had found out how to break down the atom so that atom bombs can now be produced.

But there is one flaw about this weapon, said the Germans. The bomb is so powerful that if it was used against Britain, the effects might destroy the whole world—even Germany.

So, the Germans said, the atom bomb will not be used.

I cite this item because its innocence sets the stage for a report on the battle of Stuttgart that tells of that grisly day with a bright-eyed youthful elan that may seem misplaced.

It is a letter to my wife written within a few days after Stuttgart. Some of the chipper tone may have been laid on to win Esther's admiration, and some aspects were omitted for what I considered reasons of military security. The story is still valid, but it has the theatricality and the omissions that flaw most firsthand accounts. I must therefore interpose material from my notes, from my more sober recollections and from those of my crew to lend weight to this too glib account, written by the young man I used to be.

Somewhere in England, 1943

DEAR ESTHER:

I know that I began to tell you all about the Brevet Club some days ago but I was interrupted by a bit of duty. Between then and now I have fallen into the sea and been daringly rescued, and what with one thing and another I don't feel much like rattling on about polite society at the Brevet.

The whole story is pretty melodramatic and I feel silly telling it in the first person. But, in as unpurple language as I can manage this is what happened:

The mission was the longest, the deepest penetration into Germany ever undertaken by Forts, and in talking it over among ourselves and with Carlson and the chaplain just before takeoff, I remember that I was advocating with considerable heat that this time we couldn't possibly choose to bail out or make for Switzerland or do anything but return to England because in scarcely any time at all the baby would arrive. (I've been bragging in public again.)

Just after the target we were heavily attacked. . . .

That goes much too quickly. It tells of Waterloo without mentioning Napoleon. It is altogether too bloodless a report.

Stuttgart lies some five hundred miles inside Germany. A heavily loaded B-17 flying at a moderate altitude—say, seventeen thousand feet—in formation, zigging and zagging in evasive action, might be expected to make the round trip but would land with fuel tanks perilously close to empty. There would scarcely be a gallon to spare for a foolish mistake or a bit of horseplay.

The mission was being led by Brigadier General Robert Travis. I had nothing against the General before Stuttgart because I knew very little about him except for his legendary talent at poker. After Stuttgart many of us had a great deal against him. He added to our anxieties—or at least to Bohn's—from the very inception of the mission by announcing his intention of following a newfangled theory developed by someone at Bomber Command. A great deal of fuel was being wasted by climbing to altitude with full tanks, it was reasoned. Why not climb at a later point when the tanks would be lighter?

My second-lieutenant pilot could have told the General why not, but he wasn't asked. To fly in the thin upper air a plane needs the added strength of its superchargers. If those superchargers are out of order it is best to realize that incapacity when you are over friendly territory and can drop down to a lower altitude and head for home. It is not wise to wait until one is at altitude over enemy territory to find that you cannot stay in formation.

Travis, untroubled by such technical considerations, led us across Europe at ten thousand feet until we were close to Tübingen, from which we would turn onto the target. Then he began to climb steeply and we followed him. Our superchargers worked. The record does not show whether others failed, because how can one distinguish in the fall of a Fortress the various ingredients of disaster—enemy flak or 20-mm. shells or rockets or simple mechanical failure?

We were flying low and on the outside of the formation. Travis and his lead group were in view ahead of us. As we rounded Tübingen I noted clouds moving across the Black Forest. Outside my starboard window the Neckar River was still plainly visible snaking its way to the target.

Stuttgart lay before us in checkered sun and shadow. It was close to noon. The flak came up, but not too heavy. Then as we neared the target white clouds capriciously intervened. Bob had no concerns; he would drop on the leader's bombs. But those clouds must have disconcerted Travis's bombardier, all set as he was to fix the primary target on the cross hairs of his bombsight. Could he switch at an instant from visual bombing to instruments?

We read the answer in the spectacle of our lead group passing over the target with bomb-bay doors wide open

191

and no bombs falling amid the furious black flak.

Travis was going around for another try, and the formation would wheel behind him. All very well for Travis and the happy few at the hub of that wheel. They could describe a nice, tight circle. But to us on the outward rim it meant a fearsome strain to keep up with the formation, and a serious drain of gas. We had to fly perhaps an extra forty or fifty miles at full throttle, using gas at very nearly the rate required for a takeoff, just to keep our position in the formation.

We could have come in closer to the hub, shortening the radius of the swing and saving considerable fuel, but we dared not slip under the open bomb-bay doors of Travis and his group. His bomb bays, like ours, were loaded with incendiaries. (This too seems odd, for ball bearings and the machines that make them do not burn.) The incendiaries were ingeniously pack-aged in clusters with a timing device so set that, at a predetermined distance below the bomber that hatched them, the firebombs would spread out and cover a wider area.

No one could be sure just when those incendiaries would tumble out, their clusters flying apart. We swung out in a wide arc. Why the General did not close his bomb-bay doors is yet another unanswered question of the city.

On the second time around, the incendiaries fluttered down, and smoke billowed up in black clouds from the city.

As we turned away from the target the Luftwaffe made its belated but emphatic appearance. Fighters came at us head on and blazing. Bohn was one of those pilots who believed ardently in evasive action. (There are some contrary schools of thought, which declare that it is better to fly straight and level as if on parade, following the model of the Light Brigade.) As the German planes came at us from high out of the sun, Bohn pushed *Tondelayo* to climb and pitch. This seemed to throw the attackers off momentarily. But they—or others like them—came at us again, three or four abreast. Bohn recollects that he saw a puff of smoke from the engine of one of the German fighters and in response nosed *Tondelayo* into her dance. In retrospect he much regrets that he did not accurately interpret the puff as an indication that the German pilot had cut his throttle and was waiting for us to come down from our jump while he slowed his run at us. He caught us cold and raked *Tondelayo* from nose to tail.

When he left us one of our engines was on fire; our co-pilot of the day, Chuck, had had his leg torn by a 20-mm. shell; the oxygen lines in the rear of the ship had been cut, and the oil-pressure gauge was down to zero because our oil line had been severed.

Now, it is the oil pressure that enables the pilot to change the pitch of the propellers. And if the pitch cannot be changed the propeller stands like a rigid paddle in the teeth of hurricane winds. If it spins without lubrication the friction can build up enough heat to melt metal. Then the propeller blades might turn into a deadly missile and slash the frame that held us. Our own propellers were poised like axes against us.

It was clear that we could not stay in formation. To put out the fire in our engine we would have to work up an airspeed of at least 235 mph. We could have done so only in a dive. (We had been at that deadly extremity before.) In any case we would have to drop to lower altitudes with half our crew deprived of oxygen. (We had been there before as well.)

At the first lull in the fight we waved away our wing man and dived until the fire was out.

Now we can pick up the letter to my wife.

> . . . We had to drop out of formation and fight our way across Europe by ourselves. As it developed, we didn't so much fight our way out as sneak out, running for every cloud cover we could see. The spot decision right then was up to Fawkes. He could have asked for a course to Switzerland. The lovely snowy, blue-and-white peaks of the Alps were plainly visible, towering almost up to our altitude, although quite a way off. . . .

I must interrupt again. Technically it was up to Bohn, but not actually as it turned out. Bohn was our commander—and a very good one, which is to say that he almost never gave an order. We talked this situation out, weighing the pros and cons as if we were civilians around a table. While we talked we flitted from cloud to cloud over Europe. I had given Bohn a heading, but he could scarcely keep to it while chasing clouds. I had to follow every twist and turn he made, altering our headings accordingly and still aiming for England by the shortest route.

It was plain from the most casual glance at our fuel level, at our ground speed, at our low altitude and at the distance we had to go that we could not make it back to Kimbolton. We had three choices to discuss. We could head for the Alps, where we would be interned for the duration. (General cheers over the intercom.) Choice number two: we could bail out over France. We all carried civilian passport pictures. (I liked mine because I had borrowed a very un-Army, tweedy jacket for the purpose.) We could hope to land amid the French

Resistance and follow their lead to the Channel coast, where we might thumb a ride on a fishing boat. Our intelligence captain had described this alternative as an easy walk across occupied Europe for which we were well armed with a snapshot and a .45-caliber pistol. (Dead silence for that option.)

Last possibility: we could fly as far as our fuel would permit. I told everybody I was sure we could reach the Channel. We would have to ditch, take our chances against riding down with the plane straight to the bottom of the Channel, and take our further chances on being picked up by friends, not foes, at sea. I argued for that proposal. Everyone knew it was a personal matter with me. I could see no other way to get home to my wife and shortly forthcoming child before the war's end. I might grow old while my child grew up.

"Poor Benny—he's got to see his kid." Real sympathy poured over the intercom disguised as mock tears. Bohn supported me from the start. Mike and Duke pitched in, and the others followed cheerfully.

I accepted such sacrifices without a qualm. I was young then. Would I now try to persuade others to make so risky a choice on my account? Not likely.

We knew then that our co-pilot's wounds were superficial, but would not Switzerland have seemed the safest bet for him? We could have made a case for internment. Why didn't we?

Back to the letter:

> . . . Bohn asked for a heading home and I was glad of it even though with fighting and one thing and another I was a bit vague as to our precise position at the time. We dived down into the loveliest, heaviest cloud imaginable and stayed in it as long as possible, while I feverishly worked away to

establish our position and improve on the course I
had originally set. The cloud gave out, and for a
time we sailed at low altitude over the grain fields,
forests, towns and rivers of France. Some of these
checkpoints seemed to bear out my theoretically
estimated position and some of them contradicted it.
It was beautiful country; it seemed to be of a
different color from that of England or Holland or
Belgium.

We were playing hide-and-seek in the clouds over
France. And in the open spaces our gunners were
anxiously watching for German fighters who were
looking for us but who miraculously failed to see us
before other clouds came up to hide us. However,
ground radio was tracking us and we had to shift
course to clear what I thought would be heavy flak
areas. We could see flak on both sides of us, largely
to signal fighters, we thought. . . .

At this point I must refer to Bohn, who remembers
clearly an incident which I recall only dimly. We had
been flying through cloud for some time when he asked
me where we were. He says that he could see no way in
which I could be sure of anything. And he was right, of
course. I had followed our zigs and zags as best I could,
but how could I be certain in that fog to which we clung?
Then I had my answer from the Germans. The gray-
white nothingness was punctured by black flak explosions all around us. "Ah," I said, "Rouen." We both
laughed.

. . . Just before we crossed the coast Fawkes
called up and suggested that anyone who didn't
want to take his chance in the water could still
jump. None of us did. I could see water ahead, but
we ran up along the coast to avoid a large seaport
and heavy coastal flak. Duke, our radioman, was

196

sending out an SOS and asking radio stations to take a fix on us. They did and he reported it to me, but it seemed to me to be way off. And Duke asked for another, which was just as bad. I realized then that no one in England knew where we were. I gave Duke our estimated position, but he couldn't get it through. . . .

Actually the British shore stations were asking us to move some thirty miles north where they could get a proper fix on us. They did not know it, but they were asking men to fly without wings. When we crossed the coast we had only one engine working, and in a B-17 that is a few minutes away from none. I gathered a few of my belongings—a chart of the Channel coast, which I folded and slipped into the pocket of my coveralls, a pencil or two, my gloves (gauntlet types that were more elegant than warm) and Esther's picture. Then I clambered out of the nose, up the hatch behind Bohn, and through the bomb bay to the radio room.

   . . . We were over the sea now and our four engines ran out one after another. When I left the nose, two of them were already motionless—a most disconcerting thing to see in an airplane. Back in the radio room we all took our previously assigned positions, bracing ourselves for the shock. I crouched behind the radioman's armor plating and talked to Mike, who was crouched next to me. Up to the last minute Mike retained his faith in *Tondelayo* and couldn't believe we would really have to ditch. He asked me whether we were headed toward England. I said we were but I knew we couldn't make it. We chatted like that, looking up through the open hatch to the great, gray, swirling clouds, wondering how near the water we were and when the shock would come. . . .

As we dropped closer to the sea Bohn turned to our co-pilot and asked him whether he had ever landed a plane in water. Chuck shook his head. Would he like to? No. With the last bit of power in *Tondelayo* Bohn maneuvered to land along the crest of a wave. To hit a wave broadside is very like flying into a stone wall. We skimmed the crest, then sank into the trough of a mountainous wave. We sank, then rose, buoyed by empty gas tanks.

From the cockpit Chuck saw his fondly crushed pilot's cap in the hatchway leading to the nose and seemed about to try to fish it out. Bohn recalled looking at him doubtfully as if to say, "You're on your own." No window in the cockpit of a B-17 is made to allow a grown man to wriggle out of it unless he is in the extremity of desperation. Both Bohn and Chuck made it to the wing.

Someone should have pulled a lever to release the dinghies from the fuselage. No one had. Bohn quickly scanned the directions on the metal plaque above the wing. He pulled the appropriate lever as per instructions, but nothing happened. He and Chuck pulled, twisted and clawed the dinghies out, then started the inflation, which should have been automatic. Could it have been ten seconds or thirty? None of us remembers how long it took to climb out.

> . . . We lit lightly at first and only a bit of spray seemed to come in. Mike stood up, and we all yelled to him to get down. But it was too late. After skipping along the water the ship finally plunged, throwing Mike forward so that he gashed his forehead. Then the green-gray water rushed in. I felt nothing so much as surprise. In drills there had been nothing to suggest such a torrent of ocean running through our airship. I tried to stand, but

198

the force of the water knocked me down, and when I did get up, some of the precious things I had gathered were floating.

Everyone was on his feet, everyone excited and clambering toward the hatch, everyone shouting that there was plenty of time and to keep calm. Mike stood next to me and I saw that his head was bleeding badly. A piece of floating B-17 had clipped me and scratched my forehead. For an awful moment I thought that Mike and I, who were wedged in a corner, would never get out. Mike finally managed it. By that time the water was up to my chest and rising rapidly. Our bombardier, Bob, was still in there. I hoisted myself up on one side while he made for the other. I remember that I failed to make it the first time and I could hear Mike hollering outside, "Where's Benny?" Then I clambered out. The wings were already under water.

I clung to the fuselage for a second or so and watched Fawkes and the others, who had extracted one of the rubber dinghies and were maneuvering it away from the wings of the sinking plane. Then I plunged into the water. The dinghy was scarcely more than a stroke away from the ship. But I had overlooked one detail that might have proved disastrous. I had neglected to inflate my Mae West. . . .

Actually the dinghy must have been farther off than a swimming stroke or it would have been sucked down by *Tondelayo*. Obviously a participant in an event is not the most reliable witness when it comes to precise measurements. On the other hand, the raft could not have been too far off, because I have never been a good swimmer and for that occasion I was wearing a full flying suit and boots; my pockets were stuffed with map and pencils, Esther's picture and odd bits of paraphernalia I thought I might need.

Elmer Bendiner

. . . I clung to the raft while Larry, our engineer, kept shouting, "Hold on, Benny, hold on"—as if I thought of doing anything else or going anywhere else just then. When I turned around *Tondelayo* had vanished; our dinghy and the other one holding the rest of our crew were the only things left on an apparently limitless sea. After a bit of floundering about I managed to hoist myself into the tossing dinghy. All this took much less time to live through than it does to record.

The Channel was as rough that day as it ever gets, and the swell was dark, towering and fearful to look at. It was worse to feel. We became violently seasick. That is, all except Bob and one gunner, who increased our miseries by remaining obtrusively and volubly high-spirited. There is, however, a measure of providence in the seasickness that plagues the shipwrecked. First, it gives them something to do which relieves the monotony; second; it makes death almost welcome.

Before giving way to utterly abandoned retching and writhing we paddled with our hands toward the other dinghy so that we could lash the rafts together. . . .

Dinghies are equipped with oars, but we could not find them. Eventually they turned up at the very bottom of a heap of tightly stowed, largely unworkable gadgetry.

. . . In between spasms, when I could lie with my head back and not feel too sick, I could watch the endless seascape and the barren sky. Bob was cranking our portable radio frantically but in vain, because we had lost the kite to raise our aerial; we knew then that we could send no signal at all.

From time to time Larry would bail out some of the water that swept over us in salty waves whenever we thought we might begin to dry out in the sun. Larry would bail a little, get sick, bail some more and get sick again. I tried to help, but as soon as I'd lift my head I'd vomit. I was no help at all. For five hours we tossed like that and in my lucid moments, I would speculate on the direction of our drift. It was impossible to tell with any certainty. I knew what winds had been prevailing all afternoon, but there was much I did not know. In one lucid moment I looked down at the few things I had brought with me. One of these was my Mercator's Chart. Now, darling, there is nothing quite so useless on a broad ocean as a Mercator on a raft that one cannot steer. I finally threw it overboard.

Toward the end of the afternoon we were all resigning ourselves to spending a night on the water. I, at least, was convinced that no one in England had any idea of where we were. Earlier we had seen a flight of bombers, but they were very high and no one aboard could possibly have seen our signals. It was a little more than five hours after we ditched that we sighted a squadron of fighters. Larry had the flare pistol out and ready to shoot. Duke shouted that they might be Germans. Some of us told him to shoot and others yelled at him not to. . . .

Here I must point out a rare phenomenon. Bohn said, "Fire." When Larry hesitated Bohn said for the one and only time in my memory, "That's an order." Bohn told me later that he was positive they were Spits by the sound of them, which we had heard minutes before we saw them. Actually when we spotted them they were headed like a flight of arrows to England and no one in our position—climbing and sinking amid monstrous waves—could say whether their silhouettes were German or British. They were mere specks and shadows and I could see in them neither friend nor foe. Bohn's ears for machinery were far subtler than mine. And I am grateful to them.

. . . Larry fired. The fighters were already past us, but one blessed pilot was looking back for an unknown but providential reason. We watched the fighters fly on and then noted that one peeled off, and the others followed.

They came in low over the water toward our flare—a magnificent affair of parachutes, red balls of fire and smoke like a Fourth of July celebration. Those Spitfires were the most meaningful, beautiful things I have ever seen. They swooped down and circled above us. Sick as we were, we stood up, waved and yelled at them, and came very near to upsetting the dinghies altogether. One of the Spits circled high above us to radio our position while the others continued to make passes over us by way of sustaining our morale. It was wonderful. We would cheer and laugh and get sick again, then laugh some more. I have never been so happy and so miserable at the same time.

After a while the Spits left us, but we felt certain that help would be on its way in no time at all. After a while another Spit did come out. . . .

I am reminded by my pilot that it was not a Spit but a Mosquito.

We set off another display of fireworks and he too came over to circle above us. We were very glad to have him and we were sure that we were practically saved, but the sun set and the swell seemed to grow more ominous and still there was no rescue. We knew that our guardian plane would run out of gas soon. After a final pass he left us. The moon came up, big and yellow over the water. It was a lovely night, cold but full of stars—a few of which I fruitlessly recognized—but, lovely night or no, we continued to be sick. We strained our ears listening for motors. We saw lights where there were none. We told each other that we were sure to be rescued that night. But I think that each of us acknowledged to himself that it was unlikely.

We had been in the water about nine hours when Mike suddenly shouted that he saw a light. Fawkes saw it, too, when we rode the crest of a swell. We sent up another flare and then waited. Then we heard the dull throb of a motor, and a beam of light reached out near us but not quite on us. Dinghies are pitifully small things to spot on an ocean. We fired another flare, this time into the wind so that it fell back directly over our heads. The beam swung around and picked us up. Then while the light came nearer a terrible thought struck me and most of the others, I suppose: What if the vessel were an enemy ship? To have traveled all that distance across Europe alone, to have dived *Tondelayo* into the sea, to have spent nine agonizing hours on a raft, all to avoid capture and then to be picked up by the wrong ship—that would be too bad. We shouted and soon heard someone answering. "Ahoy," said a voice behind the light. Apparently our collective Minnesota, Pennsylvania, Massachusetts, Texas and New York accents made themselves known, and the voice answered jubilantly, "OK, Yanks, we're coming."

We clambered aboard the boat, fumbling awkwardly up the swaying rope ladder. There were a dozen happy angels dressed in blue RAF uniforms and turtleneck sweaters saying, "Bloody good show," and cinematic things of that sort. They had hot soup and dry clothes ready for us. I couldn't swallow the soup and, since I paused on deck for one last mighty heave of what was still in my innards, I came down too late for the clothes. But I stripped to the skin and they wrapped me in warm fleecy blankets. . . .

While Bohn and I lingered on the deck we thought we saw a great hulk move out of the sea perilously close.

Bohn tapped the shoe of the captain on the deck above us and gestured toward it. "We've copped it," said the captain quietly, but he was wrong. The apparition was another British rescue launch, and together we headed home. The German shore batteries tossed a few shells in our direction, but they were not too serious about the effort.

. . . It was a long voyage home and we dodged minefields all the way. The skipper told us that we had drifted from our original position some twenty miles off the French coast to well within the patrol lanes of the Germans and in easy shelling distance of their coastal guns. By morning we would have been in enemy hands.

When we hit the coast town of Dover there was an ambulance waiting at the end of the stone walk. But Bendiner had no pants, nothing but a couple of blankets. I was panicky. I had read much about this town and it hurt my dignity to think that I would make my triumphal entry pantless. But I did. I clambered up the ancient stone steps of the wharf, clutching my blanket and looking like a refugee from a raid on a Turkish bath. It was very embarrassing. Those who were hurt were taken to a hospital. The rest of us—the cut on my forehead had thoroughly healed—went to the local officers' barracks of the Royal Navy, where gold-braided commodores served us rum and scotch, hot soup and bully beef. They fussed about us and sought in a thousand ways to make us happy. But still I had no pants. At last some kind lieutenant dug up an outfit for me and I regained my dignity. As a matter of fact he provided civilian clothes for me—slacks and a sweater—so that for that night and the next day I felt like a civilian and looked like Don Budge. . . .

* * *

Bohn, although a mere second lieutenant, was commander of the crew and therefore shared the quarters—and the razor—of the Admiral of the Port of Dover. He woke on the following morning to see the Admiral staring out to sea. That dignitary invited Bohn to join him for a morning dip in the Channel, then, hastily recollecting the circumstances, added, "I suppose not." Bohn confessed during our day of rehashing the events to a slight twinge of embarrassment over the fact that he had not been the last to leave *Tondelayo* in keeping with his position. I told him of the commander of the Royal Indian Navy who testified at a board of inquiry, "I did not leave the ship. The ship left me." That cheered Bohn.

On the following day, after we saw our co-pilot at the hospital and said a cheery farewell all around, our operations officer flew down to bring us back to Kimbolton. This time the groundlings had rolled our bedding and gathered our personal possessions into pathetically small packages suitably tagged. We unpacked and rejoined the living.

> . . . I expect that shortly we will be shipped off to spend a quiet recuperative week at a seaside resort. Some of the boys who have been watching me furiously pounding away have become curious, and I have shown them most of this letter. They are now anxiously waiting for the last page to roll off the press so they can find out whether or not they were saved.
>
> All my love,
> ELMER

The "quiet, recuperative week" mentioned by my young self did not come at once. We were being handled according to the latest authoritative study by Eighth Air

Force psychiatrists. A crew that had had a very rough mission a month or so earlier had been dispatched to a "flak house" for rest and rehabilitation. They came back rested but scarcely rehabilitated. They had used their week off to mull over their collective past and unpromising future. On their return they announced their unanimous decision to quit the war. They would not fly combat again together or singly. It was not mutiny, merely combat fatigue.

Colonel Mo was taking no chances with us. He and a few psychologists who had been studying combat crews to see what ordinary creatures would do under extraordinary stress decided on a policy well known to everyone who has tried to train young equestrians. If they are thrown, toss them into the saddle at once. If they have escaped a broken neck they must be encouraged to try again.

Unfortunately, Kimbolton was socked in for ten days after Stuttgart, and the dark memory of the ditching seeped into our bones while we trudged through the mud to the mess hall or down to the line to accept without joy *Tondelayo*'s replacement—a plane named *Duffy's Tavern*.

The recollection of *Tondelayo* sinking through green depths to the bottom of the Channel worked upon us. We saw our flesh within her skeleton, bloated, rising and sagging with ghastly swells, skin shredding in the eternal wash. Images teased us like sea-green sirens stirring an invitation to madness amid the autumnal swish of the fields around Kimbolton.

We did not describe to each other the atrocious look of death we ten might have worn within the twisted wreckage where our names, lettered on the metal frame, would serve as tombstones and where the flying limbs, swelling breasts and much venerated crotch of *Tondelayo* would be raped by pulsing tides and left to lie derelict.

We did not speak of her or the sea or of ourselves. I waited for a cablegram from Esther that would make me a father and seduce me from such visions. No message came for me.

We did hear from the void, though. Bohn had a note from Johnny, courtesy of the Red Cross. It was written in a breezy, wish-you-were-here mood from a *Stalag Luft*. He had floated down to earth safely but landed among people who did not recognize the war as a game. Rendered mindless by the rain of bombs or perhaps by earlier horrors, they spoke of lynching the bomb crews who came to earth. Johnny was rescued by German airmen who, in 1943, saw him as a member of their fraternity. They understood the bombing and the killing of total strangers in ways that a civilian could never appreciate. They installed Johnny safely in a POW camp where the war was quite tolerable, it seemed. He was out of it at last.

I cannot now recall whether there were any who envied him.

We came to know *Duffy's Tavern*. It was no more than a soulless collection of B-17 parts. We inhabited it as if it were a furnished room. It was serviceable but no more. And this despite some energetic efforts to pretend that it had a spirit. Duffy himself, our flyer-turned-publican, broke a bottle over its wing and we drank to it in a mood of abstracted gaiety.

We ourselves had chilled the beer for that celebration by flying a case or two up to altitude—undoubtedly the most expensively cooled beer ever consumed. I watched myself celebrate. As I recall, we all seemed to have an

207

air of odd detachment. We said and did familiar things, but I, at least, sat far back in my head, which had grown to the size of earth and heaven. I beheld myself with bemused interest while I waited word from Esther and my child.

On the sixteenth of September we piled into *Duffy's Tavern* and headed for Nantes to take yet another whack at the impervious submarine pens. We made it back with only minor damage. I believe that our nerves then had been insulated by a sheath of ice so that they carried no messages of pain or fear. Perhaps we could have finished our missions or even done many more in that strange condition, operating by mechanical reflex, beyond or beneath sensation.

However, the day after we came back from Nantes we were shipped to Blackpool as if we were machine parts that had been chipped and needed to be overhauled. We did not work our passage across England but rode as so much functionless freight. I did not regard as a luxury the situation of a passenger on a free ride. I chafed at it.

When our plane rolled to a stop and the engines were cut we leaped out on the hardstand at Blackpool. The sky was cloudless, full of the possibilities of combat. I slung my musette bag over my shoulder and waited for the others. They emerged from the waist of the plane carrying something. They gathered in a circle around whatever it was. I elbowed into the group and saw at our feet our ball-turret gunner, Leary, the youngest of the crew. His hands clutched empty air. His eyes rolled back beneath his lids, exposing a fish-white vitreous. His shirt was pulled away from his trousers, and the belt pinched the skin of his belly purple. His neck and face were splotched.

"Keep him warm . . . give him air," people shouted.

Bohn and Mike were kneeling at Leary's side. Bohn was trying to take hold of Leary's tongue to keep his airway open. Someone asked for a coat. I took mine off and handed it to Bohn, who covered Leary. Then some RAF groundlings tore up in an ambulance and loaded Leary aboard a stretcher. He too vanished as had our waist gunners on the Kassel raid, and as Johnny had earlier. Now Leary was asserting, with purple epileptic emphasis, that he would fly and fight no more. He was to go home, we learned later that day. And so he did and lived to become a cop in Philadelphia.

The rest of us, left to refresh ourselves amid the delights of Blackpool, felt our throats constrict with Leary's. We commingled our fears in long unspoken dialogues, inarticulate as the plop and twang of the lobbing of our tennis balls on the clay courts.

My mind's eye sees Blackpool as fully inhabited yet deserted like a beach resort out of season. The shops have merchandise in the window left over from a summer that has passed. Chill winds blow scraps of dead newspapers across the boardwalk. A soft malaise hangs in the air around the red-brown brick of the crenellated pseudo-Gothic castle that is the scene of our rest and recreation.

The pubs are warm and cozy, but the conversation is like the fluttering of the dead newspapers on the boardwalk. There are pretty girls in the pubs. I see them clearly, but I think I was restrained by thoughts of Esther's labor and the impending arrival of my child. Who would screw in the presence of his baby?

Bohn had his own inhibitory mechanism, and so we talked with tennis balls, plunking the gut of a racket, plopping on the clay, until we had talked ourselves out.

When we mentioned the war we talked as civilians

and strategists do, as if it were all a matter of grand movements by armies and navies, of encirclements and flanking maneuvers, of siege and statistics. The U.S. Army was battling its way inland from Salerno. Montgomery's Eighth Army was inching up the Calabrian toe. Field Marshal Rommel was flooding northern Italy with German troops to replace the wavering Italians. We could not know that Rommel even then was conspiring with the Oberburgomeister of Stuttgart to overthrow Hitler, unlock the concentration camps, construct a liberal façade and lead the Western world against Russia. If we had known, would we have spared Stuttgart to save the promising Oberburgomeister? And would we in Blackpool, concerned with our own drowned *Tondelayo* and with our odds for survival—would we have discussed such fascinating matters with the animation we can so easily muster now after thirty-five years of civilian life? I doubt it, for war is not a matter of news bulletins. It is the image of oneself inside a plane at the bottom of the sea. It is the face of an epileptic seizure. It is that shameful zest that death gives to life. It is not, assuredly, grand strategy.

Our conversation was confined to tennis sounds and the swish of curling waves on a bleak strand. We rode in a horse-drawn buggy with girls whom we caressed abstractedly. Photographers sold us snapshots of ourselves, the whereabouts of which I do not know, but I fancy that they still blow endlessly across the boardwalks of Blackpool.

It was on the last day of our rest and rehabilitation that a cablegram arrived telling me that I had a daughter. The information came complete with the usual statistics such as weight, as if she were a prize fish. Whether it was an error of transmission or my addled brain, or my unfamiliarity with babies, I do not know, but I cabled back to ask whether "14 pounds 6 ounces was good weight for one so young." We drank to her and to Esther. The crew—or what was left of it—felt, and still feel, a proprietary interest in that daughter because it was for her sake they had chosen to take their chances with the sea rather than fly to the safety of Switzerland.

I wrote my daughter a letter and another to my wife, wore fatherhood as a poppy in my buttonhole, and climbed aboard a plane sent down to fetch us home to Kimbolton.

Three days later we were over Emden, where a German battleship we had not expected to find in the harbor tossed up something like a rocket. We brought home *Duffy's Tavern* with gaping holes in wing, nose and fuselage. It was my seventeenth completed mission. Counting all the false starts and aborts it was very likely my fiftieth venture into battle. Half the original crew were no longer with us—though Mike would soon return. Three quarters of the original squadron were missing or dead or had withdrawn from combat.

I had a third of the way still to go to the magic number of twenty-five. All the military portents spoke of a bloody autumn to come.

13

By the time we returned from Blackpool the fatigue, which had settled in our bones, conferred on us a mechanical efficiency that allowed for little emotional wear and tear. We had acquired a crust that was not handsome but serviceable.

At Emden the flak had been furious, but only two crews—twenty men—were lost that day. The P-47s had been able to take us all the way because the British had provided them with auxiliary gas tanks ingeniously fabricated from paper. These had a significant advantage over the metal ones being made in the U.S.: the paper tanks were on hand and ready to fly. The others, ordered at the end of 1942, had been lost somewhere in the channels of supply. We imagined those blessed tanks accumulating in some secret warehouse beneath a Kansas wheat field or a Greenland ice floe, awaiting the signature of a bureaucrat, himself the fiction of another bureaucrat's idle brain.

On Monday morning we went to Frankfurt, where no escort could take us even with paper tanks. The Eighth Air Force lost 160 men on that trip. For three days after that the field was closed by a lid of cloud, but no passes were issued. On Friday there was a mission to Bremen and on Saturday one to Anklam and Marienburg far to the east. Our crew was not invited to those battles. I can't think why.

Some three hundred men were lost over Bremen and another 280 at Anklam. (Where were they all coming from, these offhand cowboys looking so like the offhand cowboys who had gone before them?) On Sunday we were at Münster, where another three hundred men went down to death or capture. On Wednesday we rose at the usual gray hour, had ourselves briefed, circled above The Wash for an hour and a half and then were given the message that our mission had been scrubbed. And so we groused according to our custom and faced the customary alert for Thursday, the fourteenth of October.

Sitting on the wooden benches in the briefing room at Kimbolton at four that morning, we took the news that we were going back to Schweinfurt with only a few groans to indicate that we were alive to the problem. The neophytes among us were more boisterous. Actually in the group of eighteen crews slated to represent the 379th on that mission, only four had been in the Schweinfurt battle two months earlier when we were told we were going to write history and win the war.

The spiel was more solemn this time. The message had not changed, but now the sacrifices of August recurred to mind like an insistent, muffled drumbeat beneath the text.

General Anderson sent us a personal message calling on us—not very tactfully, I fancied—to remember the blood and sacrifice of our comrades who had died on the same errand in August. We were to finish their job. Such high-toned dramatics usually read better than they play. For men like ourselves, the remnants of *Tondelayo's* crew, the message from beyond the grave sounded particularly inappropriate. It was barely arguable that those who had died some seven weeks earlier at Schweinfurt or en route had a right to cry, like Hamlet's lugubrious father, "Remember me." But we—Bohn, Bob, Larry, Duke and I—had flown with those nagging ghosts. We had gone through the fire with them and by luck had survived. Now they were using their exalted position to drive us into doing it all over again. It was easy for them to talk; they were safely dead and out of it all.

If Schweinfurt did not crumble this time or if ball bearings would continue to roll from the ruins, would there be still more ghosts to join the chorus, to call for a third, a fourth, perhaps a fifth try in their name? Obviously, with targets like Schweinfurt survival meant only a return engagement with diminishing odds.

After the call to vengeance the briefing turned to the economic, political, social and psychological significance of ball bearings. The twice-told tale was intoned like a chant. This was again the day when the German machine was to be castrated.

Mo Preston would not say that our job was to be less difficult or less costly than it had been in August. He was an honest man. He would not fly with us that day and so wore his pinks, as if it were a holiday. Little Rip Rohr was in his flying suit, energetically waving his pointer like a sword. This would be his day.

The battle plan was totally different from that of August. There would be no shuttle run. All the arguments that had been made for that experiment were now stood on their heads, but they seemed to make just as much sense that way. In August it had seemed sheer inspiration to send one division to Regensburg and thence to Africa, thereby distracting and dispersing the Luftwaffe; now it appeared that we would be in a far stronger position this time because all three hundred bombers were to go en masse to Schweinfurt.

In August it had seemed the epitome of military wisdom to attack in a long line, so that the enemy would run out of fuel and have to go down before the rear squadrons came into view. Now it seemed even wiser to concentrate all of our firepower in two massive formations that would sweep across Europe just thirty miles apart.

We humble combat flyers were not strategists. Military science seemed to me, at least, a trifle abstruse, a matter for Talmudists who can argue learnedly from any position on any question in any direction.

Our crew, with replacements, had a brand-new shiny plane, a B-17G, with twin guns in a nose turret. It was the only one of its kind on the field. No one else would have it, because its double chin was a drag in flight. It would take more power to keep in formation. Bob, however, had set his heart on those twin guns from which he could spray a more substantial shield of flying lead. Bohn gave in and requested the plane; it was given to us with scarcely an argument. The plane had a name, but I cannot now recall it. It had no soul.

Bob deserved to have his way with a whim because it was thanks to him that we no longer had to endure parachutes strapped to our bottoms which made us waddle like pregnant beetles. Bob had heard—who knows how—that there were chest chutes at an RAF base some fifty miles from Kimbolton. With one of those a man need wear only the harness and keep the chute handy. It could be snapped on quickly on one's way out of the hatch.

We flew down to the British base and had just enough time to gather the chutes. As we took off, an alert sounded, the pilots scrambled, and in another minute the field would have been closed to traffic. Now we could ride to Schweinfurt in style. We could stand upright and walk about without literally dragging our asses, as it were.

The timing was less complicated than had been called for in the August script. Two divisions were to be sent, one leaving England at Orfordness, the other farther south at Clacton-on-Sea. Together there would be about 320 B-17s. The courses of the two divisions would draw closer over the Channel so that when simultaneously they hit the enemy coast they would be thirty miles apart, creating what was hoped would prove an aerial juggernaut ablaze with some 2,500 guns. P-47s would sweep the sky before us and around us. They would go as far as their auxiliary tanks would permit, and Spitfires would wait for our return over the Channel.

We would head to Schweinfurt along a familiar path, but the route home was to lie south of our usual course out of Germany—past Metz, into Belgium and France and on to the Channel at the mouth of the Somme, just south of the Pas de Calais. We would hit England along the southern coast near Hastings.

Perhaps the experience of Stuttgart, when many of us ditched for lack of gas, had seeped into the consciousness of our chiefs. This time, though our trip would not be quite as long, we carried a spare tank in the bomb bay.

The diversionary role was assigned to sixty B-24s.

217

These were to head south and west as if to the submarine pens along the Atlantic, then continue down the coast in a long, elaborate feint designed to set the Luftwaffe scrambling on their French bases.

An English October proceeded to foul up even that simplified design. The night yielded reluctantly to a swirling dirty gray sky at the preposterously late hour of eight in the morning. The weathermen had predicted nothing more serious than a light ground mist. They assured us that we'd be out of it at 2,500 feet. We took off at about 1000, one after the other, down the runway and into the soup, spiraling upward, unseeing and invisible. We could not tell where or when or how we might meet our brothers. We were some three thousand men flying blind in a cloud bank, praying to avoid death by collision with our friends, a death that is always sad and inglorious because it is so stupid.

The "light ground mist" swirled about us at two thousand feet, was still there at three thousand, at four thousand, and at five thousand. At six thousand feet the sun began to break through the fog and bounced off the plexiglass. Then we emerged into the blue, looked around and saw a spectacle of B-17s popping through the cloud blanket and looking for their group leaders. These were firing red and green signal flares in graceful parabolas. Actually they were like hens sorting out their broods. We kept a strict radio silence. It would have been embarrassing to let the Germans hear as well as see our confusion on their radar.

Only twenty-four of the sixty B-24s got together. This was too small a force for so long and risky a diversion. They therefore flew out to the North Sea and served no purpose whatever. Most of the B-17s succeeded in form-

218

ing for the parade, although some squadrons ended up out of position, swapping high for low and head for tail. No matter. We circled for almost two hours before we achieved a full combat formation. Wheeling in the sun, I almost fell asleep.

Plainly I was growing old in combat. The anticipation of battle lifted me not quite so high as it had in earlier missions. Still, I caught my breath when from our position in the high squadron I saw again the great spectacle of a mighty fleet of Fortresses making white tracks in the blue sky, their shadows dancing over mountains of cloud below. I shook myself, fought off the chill that gripped me, scraped at the frost and told everybody that time over England was running out.

Some eighty aircraft—B-17s and B-24s—had failed to make the formation by the time we were ready to leave England. Some were lost and others had found mechanical reasons, valid or otherwise, to turn back. We were 291 Fortresses when we crossed the English coast at 1237.

Over the Channel Bob test-fired his new playthings. They boomed and clattered like jackhammers. He turned to look at me in satisfaction but not in glee. Again I saw anger on his face which I had come to know as his particular response to war. It was not anger at the enemy; only irritation at the danger, and the prevalence of death and the sense of entrapment.

The cloud cover stopped close to the English shore, and the Channel sparkled. White froth curled over the blue waves. From twenty thousand feet it was a pretty sight and I remember thinking it so at the time, although barely a month had gone by since we had mixed our bile in those waves. I do not remember imagining my bloated

219

corpse amid the wreckage of *Tondelayo* as we flew over; perhaps it is only now that I can afford such recollections.

The P-47s were around us like shining angels, all across the water and into Belgium. The flak was light over the coastal islands. It was after we had passed Aachen that our escort waggled their wings and headed back to England. Then the enemy appeared. We had spoken of them as the "yellow-nosed Abbeville kids"— those Focke-Wulf-190s, said to be Goering's favorites. They had probably been moved down from their base along the Somme, perhaps to Charleroi, perhaps to Bonn.

They came at us in waves. First were the familiar yellow-noses, two, three and four abreast, flying in at twelve o'clock. It was after they had gone that the fancy work began. Rockets exploded precisely at our level. I am told that these were lobbed by two-engine fighter-bombers from above and to our rear. They carried their launchers under their wings and, after they let go, transformed themselves into fighters. I saw them careening down the plexiglass of my window.

After them came new waves of rocket launchers. Stuka dive bombers plummeted on us like falcons on field mice. Perhaps I put the case too strongly. Bob was drilling the air from his chin turret so that the nose compartment was filling up with eye-smarting gunpowder fumes. Surely some field mice were killing falcons.

Again I noted everybody's kills—from the tail, the waist, the belly. I recorded the place, the time, the altitude. I observed the rockets, the flak and the puffs of cloud. I jotted down the second that the city of Bonn slipped by the starboard window. (It was a red-roofed town, seemingly quiet beneath that unquiet sky.)

Then I began to note the landmarks of a nightmare. As in August there were the yellow blazes among the rectangular patches of landscape, like bonfires in a field. I clocked the fall of Fortresses and, when someone sang out the number of parachutes that opened, I tried to keep a score. But I never pretended that I could be precise at such a time, with the mask sitting on my nose, with the tin pot on my head and frost blotting out my view.

As we came up on Schweinfurt smoke began to drift across the city. The fighters backed off to let the ground batteries have their way with us. From above, below and all around came the rattle of shrapnel. I noted: "Flak intense." The bomb-bay doors in the planes up ahead swung open. Bob had opened ours and now kept his finger on the toggle switch to let our load go down with the others.

When the bombs were gone we banked sharply to starboard and at once ran into an enemy storm. Never had we seen so many Germans in the sky at one time, and never had their attacks seemed so well coordinated. Adolf Galland, in charge of the German fighter arm, later wrote that he had been able to concentrate on our planes virtually the entire strength of the Luftwaffe's defending forces. There were, he said, some three hundred day fighters along with forty fighter-bombers and night fighters. They came from all over Germany and even from the Third Fleet off France.

They went down, gassed up and rose again to intercept us repeatedly along our course. In fact there were two or three fighters available for every one of our bombers. Wherever one looked in the sky there were Germans attacking, and B-17s smoking, burning, spinning down. One German fighter, perhaps hit and out of control, could not perform the usual stylish backward flip and instead crashed into the wing of a B-17—one of our group it was—and the two planes burst into a single ball of fire. Streaming smoke and flame, inextricably intertwined, they tumbled down to the tilled checkerboard.

Galland does not say by what means he was able to mobilize all this might against our formations. American historians have speculated that perhaps German intelligence had picked up the pillow talk of the high Brass. (It would be far too much to hope that all the whores of England were on our side.) No probe has ever revealed the leak, and high American officers say no more than that too many people knew of the Schweinfurt mission.

Although at the start of the war German air intelligence was in the hands of overaged civil servants and retired policemen, whose most advanced equipment consisted of binoculars, by the time of Schweinfurt it had become a triumph of technological wizardry and futuristic theatricality. In bunkers jocularly called "battle opera houses" the high command gathered before huge panels of frosted glass on which the battle appeared in spots of light and an illuminated script. With a lag of barely a minute, the precise status of each squadron, perhaps each plane—ours and theirs—was depicted on the battle panel. The data were fed to the apparatus by hundreds of reports from radar stations, from planes in combat or on reconaissance, from ground observers and from a host of other sources.

Describing the swarm of personnel inside the "opera house" dashing about in a haze of cigarette smoke, Galland was reminded of "a huge aquarium lit up, with a multitude of water fleas scuttling madly behind the glass walls." The command post was in the balcony, where those in charge of the fighters and fighter-bombers dispatched them in orders that were instantly transmitted to ground or air personnel.

It is strange to consider that each burning plane I saw, each torn wing, each maneuver of my own craft, was recorded—not as the fall of the proverbial sparrow is noted in heaven, but as an illuminated symbol on a screen in an underground theater at a matinee performance.

I do not know how our homeward journey appeared on that panel, which, for all its drama, lacked the flesh and smell of reality, but for us it seemed an endless run through a terrible maze. At each corner of the maze a body burned. No one could trace the human features in the fire or the charred fragments of uniform and flesh that dropped from the image. You saw yourself in the flames and passed on. Across Germany, across Belgium, across France in the fast-falling dusk, amid lowering clouds ran the trail of fires—ghostly flares lighting an infernal landscape with no horizon, no sun and no shadows. The earth was no longer tilled land. The cities were empty and staring. One imagined a world of grotesque fungi. The only signs of animation appeared in the yellow flicker of burning B-17s.

It was sometime that afternoon that Albert Speer was conferring with Hitler in East Prussia. An adjutant interrupted them to say that Goering was on the phone with cheery news. We, or those of us who had fallen, were the glad tidings. Hitler reportedly returned to the meeting, beaming over the great German "victory" in the making.

At Aachen there were no P-47s to meet us and see us

223

safely home. An October cloud had settled over England and kept them from our rendezvous. We pressed on amid the drone of our engines, the chatter of our guns and the pinging of flak on our belly, lonely except for the sight of other machines in that inhuman sky.

When we came up on England south of London we were in a gray shroud. Rohr waggled his wings to say that we were on our own. We made our way west of London, taking no chances on exciting British flak. We flew low enough so that I could trace the Thames winding to Windsor over the dark hills near Berkhamstead. I picked up a railroad that I thought would run northwest to Luton, but the mists kept Luton from me. We passed spires and fields which, in the dust and fog, were indistinguishable from a thousand other English fields and spires. I found the River Ouse looping around Bedford and we were almost home. We passed the little airdrome at Risely, then the castle of Kimbolton, and at last our field. The ceiling was barely above the treetops. I packed my maps. The rest would be up to Bohn, and I had not a second's doubt that he would bring us in.

Only a few of us landed that night at Kimbolton. Survivors of the second Schweinfurt were scattered all over England. Some had come down at the first airfield they spotted through the fog. Some had landed in potato patches. Some crashed.

Bohn, usually so charitable even to high Brass, had harsh words for Rip Rohr because he had left his troops to flounder in the muck of an October fog. It was pleasant for a navigator to feel indispensable, but perhaps it was more important for us all to be angry, to snarl at Rip and at the weather. Anger is more therapeutic by far than love or charity.

224

Of our group of eighteen that had started from Kimbolton that morning, only three or four had come home that night. Others straggled in the next day until the number of survivors came to twelve. Six of our planes were burned-out hulks somewhere in Europe, and sixty men would be listed as missing.

The overall percentage for the Eighth Air Force was only marginally better. Of the 291 crews that crossed the Channel, 29 were lost before they reached the target, another 31 fell on the way home—60 in all, 600 men missing out of a force of less than 3,000. The loss was greater than one out of every five. In six days of warfare we had lost 1,480 crewmen over Europe. It was impossible to endure the continued decimation.

One measure of our losses was the extraordinary shipment of laurel wreaths that arrived from on high. Winston Churchill checked in with an eloquent message "on our magnificent achievements." General Marshall told us of our "brilliant, punishing blows." Air Chief Marshal Portal expressed "deep admiration." To Hap Arnold it seemed unaccountably clear that we were "moving toward supremacy in the air." Eaker expressed his "unbounded admiration," and Colonel Mo had all of these encomia mimeographed, stapled in bouquets and sent to each one of us with his own covering words of pride.

Still, it was evident that the war was not grinding to a halt, that the German machine was not about to collapse in a heap for lack of Schweinfurt ball bearings. Though the question did not agitate us at the time, it may now be asked whether in fact we had vindicated Billy Mitchell.

14

Our bombing was a good deal better in October than it had been in August, according to the definitive survey of bomb damage. We hurled down on Schweinfurt a total of 395 tons of high explosives and 88 tons of incendiaries. The accuracy of the incendiaries was hard to estimate, but of the 1,122 high-explosive bombs we let fly, 88 scored direct hits on those factory buildings designated as prime targets, and 55 other bombs landed within the factory area, wreaking extensive damage.

Speer writes that after receiving the news of a German "victory" he hurried off to check on what we had done to Schweinfurt. Telephone wires were down, but he succeeded in putting through a message over the police wire to the foreman of one of the ball-bearing factories. That observer reported that all three of the principal factories had been very badly hit and, to make matters worse, the oil bath prepared for the bearings had caught fire. He estimated that the August raid had knocked out ten percent of bearing production. This one probably would cost the Germans 67 percent, pending repairs. (Had our planners really known about the oil bath and calculated the effect of incendiaries? Not likely, I think; it was a piece of luck.)

The center of the city was on fire from some of our misplaced incendiaries. Some three hundred civilians had perished, but almost a third were estimated to be foreign "slave labor." When these figures were produced long after the event, twenty-six children were counted among the dead.

Based on the logs of the navigators who returned, and allowing very rough discounts for duplication, uncertain sighting, lack of confirmation, and plain lying, General Eaker released to the press his estimate of enemy losses: Of 300 fighters put up against us, 99 were definitely shot down. (The Germans put their losses at 25.)

If one took Eaker's estimate more seriously than it deserved, the enemy loss was far greater than our own. The bombing of Schweinfurt thus appeared to be costly but not extravagant. Moreover, it was explained, we could replace machines and men at a faster rate. (Perhaps, but surely it was easier to replace one small fighter manned by one pilot than to turn out a very complex bomber with a crew of ten.)

Arnold asked Eaker to rush to him all evidence of our inevitable victory. According to Thomas M. Coffey, a chronicler of Schweinfurt and particularly of Eaker's role in that battle, the General answered that request in these words:

> I feel there is much evidence in the direction you are inquiring. Yesterday's effort was not, as might at first appear, contrary thereto. I class it pretty

much as the last final struggle of a monster in his
death throes. There is not the slightest question but
that we now have our teeth in the Hun Air Force's
neck.

So did Eaker whistle as he passed the graveyard of the
Eighth Air Force in the dark of the moon. In Washington
Arnold told the press, "Now we have got Schweinfurt."
Few experts in Washington or elsewhere were actually
convinced, and President Roosevelt declined to describe
Schweinfurt as a great victory.

The reconaissance photos nevertheless gratified Major
Perera and the Committee of Operations Analysts, who
must be credited with the original inspiration for the
assault on Schweinfurt. A memorandum from the COA
dated October 25, 1943, urged a prompt follow-up:

The successful attack on Schweinfurt has unquestionably already caused the enemy to take measures of various types to protect the ball-bearing
supply. The longer additional attack is delayed, the
more effective those measures can become . . . if
delayed sufficiently long the additional attack will
produce only a staggered loss of production, not the
desirable concentration of loss.

It was plain to everybody—German, Briton and American—that we ought to hit Schweinfurt again within a
week or two at the outside, but at that moment the Brass
could scarcely risk the effect on the public of another
catastrophe.

Decades after the war Eaker went to Heidelberg for a
chat with Albert Speer, who by then had served his term
at Spandau for his service as Hitler's armaments wizard
and was profiting from his published confessions. In that

conversation, as printed in *Air Force Magazine,* Speer commented, "At first I was most worried about ball bearings. If you had repeated your bombing attacks and destroyed our ball-bearing industry the war would have been over a year earlier. Your failure to do so enabled us to get bearings from Sweden and other sources and to move our damaged ball-bearing machines to dispersed localities."

That view of Speer's is confirmed in the semiofficial American history *The Army Air Forces in World War II,* by W. E. Craven and J. L. Cate, who maintain that in the four months following the second battle of Schweinfurt the Germans were able to reorganize the ball-bearing industry "so thoroughly that any further effort to destroy it was doomed to failure."

However, there are grounds for suspecting that even such authoritative historians as Craven and Cate may have succumbed to a tendency common in democratic observers to magnify the efficiency of the Nazi regime. Speer offers the most convincing testimony against Craven and Cate and against his own declaration to Eaker. In his memoir *Inside the Third Reich,* Speer makes it clear that although he had been advocating dispersal of the ball-bearing industry since December 1942, very little was done about it until the middle of 1944.

The local gauleiters, he explains, were opposed to setting up new plants in the countryside because it would bring the war to their hitherto peaceful districts.

After the August battle of Schweinfurt there was talk of dispersal but no action. After October's raid, meetings were held and solemn decisions formulated, but still little or no active steps were taken. In January 1944 the matter was still under discussion, and in August of that year Speer's subordinates were still complaining of difficulties in "pushing through the construction work for the shift of ball-bearing production."

If the Germans did not disperse their ball-bearing plants for almost a year after Schweinfurt, why didn't our strategic bombers destroy those all-important facilities and shorten the war by at least a year and some thousands of lives? Certainly, once the range of Allied fighter escorts was extended by auxiliary tanks in 1944, we could have raided Schweinfurt without inordinate losses. And we did, particularly in February and March of 1944.

Yet the ball bearings continued to roll. How? Why wasn't the German war machine a smoking shambles, consumed by its own friction? Why did German tanks, planes, trucks and guns continue to come off the assembly lines in ever increasing numbers?

Those very questions were addressed in a meeting of Major Perera's Committee of Operations Analysts in June 1944. According to the minutes, a Major I. F. Stark of Air Corps Intelligence remarked, "There isn't an awful lot you can do to the machinery. It can be repaired rapidly. A great deal can be brought in from outside machine shops. . . ."

Asked by various members of the high Brass in attendance at the meeting just how much of the machinery would have to be destroyed for a raid on a ball-bearing factory to be considered effective, the major answered, "I can only guess. I would keep it [production] below the forty percent level."

"Has our past bombing brought it down to forty percent?" a colonel wanted to know.

Stark answered, "No, sir, the lowest was about fifty percent."

Then there occurred an exchange which to the survivors of Schweinfurt has a soul-corroding irony. A colonel brooded aloud on the intelligence estimate he had just heard: "That would indicate to me that bearings are not a critical item."

And the intelligence major answered: "I have guessed enough, sir."

Actually the major gave up too easily. The guessing game has gone on for decades. Curtis LeMay, when still a colonel but already disenchanted with our performance at Schweinfurt, declared: "This operation was the outgrowth of a search by those intellectual souls in Plans and Intelligence to find an easy way of winning the war in Europe. That's just about like a search for the Fountain of Youth. There is no such thing; there never was. But they were trying to find it and they hit on bearings."

The logic behind the selection of the ball-bearing plants as the key to victory was so neat and tempting that one can understand the enthusiasm of our master strategists. They cannot be condemned merely because they—and we—failed.

Other more troublesome questions arise, however. Wasn't it abundantly clear that we could not hope to demolish Schweinfurt in a single assault? And didn't we also know in advance that we had not the resources for a series of assaults on the city? Why, then, did we go ahead and suffer the expected staggering losses when we knew we lacked the means to complete the job?

Speer asked Eaker that same question in their conversation at Heidelberg.

Speer: "I have often wondered why you began your bombing attacks with such limited forces. Would it not have been better to have waited until

232

you had several hundred or perhaps a thousand bombers available?"

Eaker: "We did not have that option, for several reasons. After Pearl Harbor, there was great pressure both at the political level and among the military leaders to send all our bombers against the Japanese . . . it was only by demonstrating as early as possible that the daylight bombing offensive against Germany was feasible and productive that we were able to sustain our bomber buildup for operations out of Britain as originally planned. . . ."

Eaker continued his remarkable explanation:

"Here is another consideration you may not have taken fully into account. Armies and navies have clashed for centuries, and their battles, strategies and tactics have been recorded, studied and analyzed by historians and war colleges of many nations. Prior to World War II, air power had never had similar experience. Although Lord Trenchard of Britain, General Douhet of Italy and General William Mitchell of the U.S. had prophesied that strategic air power could exercise a decisive influence on warfare, those theories had never been tested . . .

"For the first time the U.S. Eighth Air Force, operating out of Britain, and Britain's own Royal Air Force were to be given the resources to test those theories of the use of strategic air power. General H. H. Arnold, head of the U.S. Army Air Force, was a dedicated Mitchell disciple. His instructions to General Carl Spaatz and to me were clear cut, specific, unmistakeable. We were to take the heavy bombers General Arnold would send us and demonstrate what air power could do. . . ."

*   *   *

My civilian mind finds it difficult to follow such military footwork, but I try. We were sent on a hazardous mission to destroy in a single day an objective that was vulnerable only to repeated assaults for which we had not the strength. Those objectives could not wait for the arrival of more bombers, of the promised Mustangs, of belly tanks and wing tanks, because we had to dramatize the importance of air power in the European Theater for the benefit of the public and the Navy.

If that is a fair reading of our commander's thought processes, then Schweinfurt's ghosts must ride with those of the Light Brigade at Balaklava—brave soldiers forever charging to their deaths in gallant absurdity.

But that is not the sum total of our reckoning. Although the war was certainly not won, nor even measurably advanced, at the battles of Schweinfurt, those missions were part of a larger and very significant air assault on Europe. Speer declares: "The real importance of the air war consisted in the fact that it opened a second front before the invasion of Europe. That front was the skies over Germany."

For a while in 1943 and 1944 our chiefs had the mistaken notion that the ever increasing waves of German fighters seen in western skies had been brought from the Russian front. Actually those fresh planes were being turned out by German factories which had increased their production despite our bombing. Our intelligence officers were all the more impressed by the Luftwaffe's vigorous capacity for self-renewal because we tended to believe that our own kill claims were exaggerated by a factor of only two when ten would have been closer to the truth.

Nevertheless, it is certainly true that the Eighth Air Force was tying down at least 900,000 Germans and some 10,000 pieces of artillery in air defense, according to the top Brass of the Reich. "Without this great drain on our manpower, logistics and weapons," Speer says, "we might well have knocked Russia out of the war before your invasion of France."

We were then instrumental, perhaps decisive, distractions in the battle for Russia. A few years ago Bomber Harris went to High Wycombe to unveil a plaque marking the spot where planners dispatched "gallant aircrews to the enemy's heartland." He took the occasion to declare as "incontrovertibly proved" the thesis that strategic bombing "won by far the greatest land victory of the war . . . won by far the greatest air victory of the war . . . won by far the greatest naval victory of the war." Citing Speer and other German sources, he credits our second front in the air with victory on the eastern front, although if pressed he would no doubt acknowledge the assistance of the Red Army. He also notes the testimonials from General Sepp Dietrich, German commander at the Ardennes, who complained that his troops could no longer endure the heavy bombing; from Eisenhower, who acknowledged that the Air Forces had "achieved the impossible"; and from Montgomery, who said that the bombers "did more than anybody toward winning the war."

Those are handsome endorsements, but the examples of air power they cite seem to be more tactical than strategic. In opposition to the fervent wishes of Billy Mitchell and his defenders, the air arm was still being wielded to assist an attack by land.

When Harris talks about Allied victory in the air he can summon up more solid evidence. While *Tondelayo*'s crew was struggling to survive in 1943 the Germans had undeniable superiority; when D Day came the Allies had it. Eisenhower could then promise the troops that any plane they might see over the Normandy beaches would be friendly. Actually, not a single German plane harassed the Normandy landings on June 6, 1944.

If the Luftwaffe had been as strong in June as it had been the previous November the invasion might never have come off. Surely much of the credit is due to the Eighth Air Force. Still, it was not strategic bombing that redressed the balance in the air. German fighter planes were still being turned out in adequate numbers despite our attack on aircraft factories. The trouble was that Germany was running out of aircrews. The claims of downed Focke-Wulfs and Messerschmitts which in 1943 had been made out of blue sky, boyish enthusiasm and overheated PR were approaching accuracy in 1944. German losses rose as Allied fighters lengthened their range.

There again we airmen of '43 had demonstrated in our own flesh and blood the fallacy that a formation of heavily armed bombers, alone and unescorted, could triumph over any swarm of fighters. What a pity that theories of war cannot be tested in a laboratory with flying guinea pigs.

Of course, there were other factors besides air superiority that account for the success of the Allied invasion. Hitler's dunderheadedness was one. For days he had insisted that the Normandy landing was no more than a feint, a transparent ruse which only his mind had been able to detect.

(This illusion was probably nurtured by "disinformation" dropped into his official news sources by Allied agents. Actually Hitler had correct reports of the place, time and hour of the invasion, but he scorned such intelligence as planned deception and would not even transmit it to Paris.) Hitler was also under the impression that flak was far deadlier than German fighters. I have often wondered what clever agent dropped that fallacy into his ear. He actually ordered fighter production stopped in favor of flak batteries, but these orders were apparently sidestepped by the adroit Speer.

Harris noted that thirty-seven Allied divisions containing "a large proportion of green, untried and inexperienced troops swept sixty-one German defending divisions clean across Europe from the Atlantic to the Elbe, destroyed the German Seventh Army of half a million men, captured hundreds of thousands of prisoners and all their materiel and beat them down to total defeat and surrender." All this he attributed to Allied victory in the air.

He went on to claim the triumph of air power over sixteen of the eighteen mightiest ships of the German High Seas Fleet. He promised that the lesson to be learned from sea versus air power "will be finalized in the Atlantic in the next war."

I sympathize with Harris and the other academicians of war. They were frustrated in 1943 by the primitive resources at their disposal. We aircrews would not match their vision of neat and precise destruction. We missed too often, and too many of us died. We were inept and perishable. It would be gratifying to add that we were also handicapped by inconvenient moral scruples not usually found in aircraft components, but such a suggestion would be transparent foolishness. Some commentators who now speak of our bombing offensive as a "children's crusade" magnify beyond recognition the purity of our souls while they downgrade our intelligence.

We were not children fired with a vision—our own or

that of others. We were not escaping from villages too cramped and tedious for our adolescence—although that is an incidental benefit to be derived from almost any calamity. We were merely young men accepting our times. Some of us fancied the roles we played; others did not. In any case we did not go off into the sky shouting hosannas.

Even now, edging past middle age, few of us, I believe, awake in sweat because of the German civilians whom we have blasted. If war dreams disturb us, it is because they replay old fears from which we wake to ward off our own deaths, not the deaths of others.

It has become fashionable for every postwar generation to dissect the glories that went before them. I think that is wholesome if done with a degree of taste and a respect for the nuances of history. Heroes, like house pets, should never be overpowering. But a healthy skepticism is not quite the same as the cultivated mannerism of disillusion. I cannot take seriously those who adopt the pose of the disenchanted without having experienced the prerequisite enchantment.

World War II had less starry-eyed enchantment than most wars. We were not gulled by slogans. Hitler was real and his victory had to be prevented. For many of us that was the only point of the war. Critics aspiring to the melancholy glamor of membership in a "lost generation" will grant that truth but nevertheless insist that our means—the setting of fire storms in crowded cities, for example—fatally besmirched our ends.

Yet a question nags me: Suppose our leaders were pure in heart and dedicated solely to the destruction of fascism, undistracted by lesser ambitions, not caring whether the Air Forces or the Navy won the war so long as it was won; and suppose that their minds were as brilliant as their hearts were pure, and that the blasting of cities was in fact the only key to victory; then would not the sacrifice of thousands of lives have been worth it? If one can practice a terrible and Godlike arithmetic, can we say that we were right to kill thousands because they number less than the millions who would have died or lived appallingly if Hitler had won? Could we have dared to refrain from such a sacrifice merely to keep our hands clean? Admittedly this is a dangerous kind of bookkeeping, for if we allow it who can say that any terror is not justified in a cause we believe to be good? And if after the killing discerning critics point out that the strategists were not pure in heart or particularly wise and that therefore some of our victims died needlessly, where can we find absolution? Only in this: that our cause was just. This sets us apart from our enemies.

I am not an absolutist who would follow a logical road to hell. I would indeed draw lines and maintain that some sacrifices are not acceptable even in a just cause. I would not have dropped an atom bomb even to wipe out Hitler, because the bomb makes possible the end of all life. We carried no such heavy freight in our B-17s. We carried death for ourselves or for others, but humanity was not doomed in the fall of Fortresses.

15

War cannot be contained in the cerebrations of military strategists. The chess master who designs a war is comparable to the architect of a theater. He furnishes the stage for wonders he cannot imagine. The truth of war is more elusive and multifaceted than that of the theatrical or religious arts. Like these art forms war requires a commitment and a self-abandonment; it thrives on discipline, demands sacrifice and is not easily defined. Unlike the arts, war is most shameful when it is most glorious.

My final days in combat over Germany had in them a mixture of shame, anguish and the ludicrous that says something concerning the nature of my particular war.

It was almost a week after Schweinfurt that we went off to Düren, a center for the metal industry southwest of Cologne. I cannot recall precisely what happened, but about half the force of 212 bombers never made it to the target. Only nine planes were actually downed, I hasten to say, since the enemy was busy chasing his tail and seemed even more confused than we were.

As we crossed the enemy coast we began unrolling long strands of silver-colored paper. We called the device "window" and the British called it "chaff." The streamers were very pretty as they spiraled down in the sun. They were designed to clutter up the German radar screens and they did the job superbly, as German accounts of the Düren raid subsequently revealed.

From Holland to the Ruhr, radar stations mistook our "window" for vast armadas on the wing. The fighter stations, experienced in such illusions, disregarded their screens and turned to other sources of information. Fortunately for us, Goering took a personal hand that day. He was spending the morning at home in Karinhall, his luxurious estate near Berlin. It was there that he hung looted European art treasures row upon row as if they were snapshots in an album or trophies of a hunt. (He saved a second-rate but lubricious figure of a nude Europa to enhance the attractions of his oversized canopied bed.) He also maintained at Karinhall a radar screen with all the concomitant communications apparatus he might need should he wish to take over the air war while still in his pajamas.

On that October day he flashed a message to all posts: "The Reichsmarschall is taking control." He had decided that, contrary to what the fighter stations had decided, the Americans were on their way back to Schweinfurt. He therefore dispatched dozens of fighter squadrons to the ball-bearing city.

He was absolutely certain that he was right when listening posts reported hearing sounds of air fleets above the overcast near Schweinfurt. Then the sounds seemed to go past the city. The Americans were going on to Leipzig, Goering figured, and he ordered his planes in pursuit.

Tracking them by sound, Goering dispatched additional squadrons to Pilsen. Then, as the clouds broke, the Germans saw their skies filled with German planes scurrying from place to place at Goering's orders, chasing an invisible enemy. Meanwhile we had been to Düren, dropped our bombs and headed home. Our losses had been less than ten percent, almost acceptable in the eyes of our commanders.

November days grew shorter, colder and meaner. They seemed scarcely more than intervals of gray murk between sunrise and sunset. An anxiety began to gnaw at my stomach. I was nearing my twenty-fifth. I wanted to go home to Esther and my daughter, but they were in a world so remote that I could regard them only as images in a travel brochure of faraway fantasies.

Certainly I wanted to survive my twenty-fifth. And yet, fluttering my intestines was the thought that for me something was ending; death was fading away and would not play with me again. I am now giving that dark fancy an expression. Then it was inchoate and I did not seek to define it.

We fought at Wilhelmshaven and at Bremen in such magnificent fleets that again I had the illusion of invincibility. We crossed the Channel with five hundred bombers and hundreds of fighters. Our commanders were experimenting with an elite approach to navigation. "Pathfinders" were to be trained and equipped for lead positions. I was too close to the end of my missions to be considered for such an assignment. I was as wistful as a boy who sees boyhood becoming more attractive while he prepares to grow up.

I am certain that few of those who genuinely suffered

in the war ever looked back wistfully to their agonies. Did any infantryman leave the jungles of New Guinea with a mesmerized backward look at the mud, the insects buzzing over suppurating wounds, the boredom broken only by occasional shells? Perhaps. And I do not even presume to guess the thought of those who walked out of Dachau.

I do not think I would have had those oddly mingled emotions that November if what was left of the original crew were to finish together. But Duke and I had occasionally filled vacancies on other crews and so would reach our twenty-fifth before Bohn and Bob and Larry and Mike. They would have to stay behind while we, sporting our decorations, could go out among the paddlefeet of the strange world beyond Kimbolton.

My twenty-fifth came on November 29. It was our second visit to Bremen in three days. We climbed through soup and emerged into a blue sky lit by a sun that shed no warmth. The chill ate into my ribs and goaded my frostbitten toe to ache with the memory of its earlier insult. I scrunched my arms into my sides, barely lifting them to chip the frost from the window. There were about 150 planes in our parade; other formations were en route elsewhere to north Germany. (We looked brave out there, but with the Schweinfurt losses still in headlines our chiefs dared not send us beyond the reach of P-47s and the Mustangs which were appearing for the first time in our theater, though without wing tanks that would make the difference in later months.)

With our fighters fanning out around us and above us we looped far out over the North Sea before turning to make our run to the target. A frontal system, visible in a line of towering stratocumulus, lay between us and Bremen. We passed over the clouds and noted the edge of the front on the thermometer that tracked the outside temperature. It began to rise, though it was still no more than sixty below zero Fahrenheit.

As we turned toward the target the windows frosted into dazzling snowy pinpoints of light, blinding the view. In the nose Bob and I could barely see blue sky and distinguish the shapes of fighters. Ours or theirs? We could not tell. We tracked them with our guns but did not fire.

We could not know it at the time, but the cockpit was then in real trouble. The window defroster had failed in the stress of the frontal passage. The engines may hum, the props spin, all the intricate nerves of a plane may function superbly, but the failure of a simple defroster can prove fatal.

In that bitter cold of 25,000 feet in November over the North Sea, Bohn had to open his window and put his head out to see where he was going. In a hurricane of lacerating cold he had to keep from blinking so that his tears might not freeze his eyes shut.

We saw a German pop up through a solid blanket of clouds beneath us. It was an ME-109. Bohn saw him, too. We watched him far out, maneuvering for a head-on attack. He was coming in. Bohn called us on the intercom and his voice was strained. Bob turned to me his eyes blazing. He banged a fist on his gun. Was it jammed, or what? He pushed me aside to try my gun, though it could not be swiveled far enough to catch the oncoming fighter in its sight. There was no click, no chatter. The gun was dead. Bohn called again and again to fire. Our plane was silent. Our guns, in that brief passage from cold to warmer, moister air, had frozen.

I turned to look at the other planes of the formation. Not a tracer flew. The Messerschmitt came on. He was

well within range now and we had not a gun to stop him.
Could he then rake the formation, burn us to the ground,
because the damned sky had made us impotent as hens
mesmerized in the presence of a fox?

Then we noted that no lights were playing along his
wings where we knew his guns should be firing. He came
through the squadron up ahead and no planes fell. He
passed us at our level, and Bohn, who had a better view
than I had, says he waved. Bohn says he had a black
mustache; he saw the enemy that clearly at the moment
when a meteorological happenstance imposed a truce.
An inversion—with cold air below the clouds and com-
paratively warm air above—had momentarily sealed his
guns.

I do not recall the enemy's mustache or his farewell
wave, but I saw him turn and plunge downward into the
gray rolling clouds.

Minutes later in stable air the guns thawed. We could
again be as murderous in our defense as need be. We
bombed Bremen through the overcast and the flak. On
the way home German fighters came up in force. They
and the flak knocked out of the sky thirteen of our planes
carrying 130 men. I was not among that number, and it
had been my twenty-fifth.

I smiled when I was congratulated. I got off a letter to
Esther. That night and all the next day I felt curiously
disembodied. I was there and not there. I walked the
same roads I had always walked. I slept where I had
always slept, but all was changed. I was not part of my
crew. I watched them go about their work and their
preparations in my absence. They would talk about
getting together with me sometime if . . . We would see
each other in London, New York, Minneapolis, Boston,
if . . .

THE FALL OF FORTRESSES

I no longer shared that highly charged existence in the shadow of the if. I would learn to live as I had once lived without that omnipresent, stimulating shadow. True, I had never forsaken my childish belief in invulnerability, but nevertheless the if had always been there, on the other side of my plane's window, peeking from behind Esther's picture, within the envelope of her letter. I became attached to it. I felt that somehow the conditional lent a distinction to life. One must indeed be hungry for distinctions to develop a fondness for that grinning, gap-toothed conjecture of death.

I confess, nevertheless, that I had grown accustomed to that presence as the eleventh member of the crew, and I would miss him along with the others. The feeling of impending separation grew keener on the evening of November 30. The field was alerted. My crew would fly and I would not. I had been offered a job at Wing Headquarters, helping to design missions for others. It would have meant a captaincy and a job in a world of pleasant mess halls, staff cars and jeeps, with just enough time in an airplane over Britain to collect my flying pay. I had turned it down for a chance to go home, see Esther, meet my daughter and, pending assignment to some other war, live the life of those who need no poppy in their buttonhole to assure survival.

I was sure that I wanted such a life as any sane man would. A part of me was sane and had sane desires. A better-organized army would have rushed me off the base within the very hour I had completed my twenty-fifth. I should have vanished as definitively as those who die or resign from combat. Perhaps my decision to forgo the promotion and opt for home had upset some part of the machinery. In any case I had been told that I was not to go home for a while at least. I would have to do a stint of teaching navigation to neophytes in Northern Ireland.

"Ireland?" echoed Joyce and her mother in a concerted wail of disbelief. I had gone to see them in the afternoon to say goodbye. To the Woffords of England, Ireland was the utmost edge of the world, a place of terrible exile. I scuttled their sympathy with laughter and rolled Joyce's farewell kiss upon my tongue. Then I came home to the field, the alert and a sense of desolation.

I remember the bar in the officers' club. The wood was blond and highly polished. It ran the entire length of a very long wall, or so it seems to me in recollection. A mirror was hung behind it on which was pasted a collection of decorous breasts, legs and toothy smiles. There was a crude cardboard facsimile of our emblem—crossed bombs and death's head.

Blackout curtains covered the windows. No one sat at any of the tables near the stoves. The place was cold, as I remember, and empty. I do not think there was a soul there except myself. Someone must have been tending bar, but I do not recall a face or a name or a word that was exchanged. I think there was a yellow light over the bar, but most of the room was in semidarkness.

I stood with my foot on the rail. I drank a scotch and soda. I do not recall another time throughout the war that I drank alone. I usually drink to keep in step or to ease the flow of talk. That night of the alert I must have been groping for words to say to myself, desperate to find something to do while the others slept the uneasy sleep that waits for the glare of a flashlight, for the grumbling and the whining, and the start of a new mission in the deadly cold sky.

Would I wake at that summons, turn over and go back to sleep? Would I haunt the mess and the flight line like a damned ghost? How stupid, how cruel to let me stay

alive and safe among those who are still hostages to
death. No surgeon would leave an amputated limb near
the living patient. It should be taken away, put out of
sight, allowed to regenerate a body as a worm does when
it is severed.

I do not remember a man coming into the bar, but
there he was next to me. I have forgotten his name. He
was a PR man—an information officer. I had known him
slightly, and occasionally given him a bit of color to
adorn a press release. He was a mild-mannered man, one
of many I had known on the field as I knew the color of
the bar or the turn of the road. Until that moment he
had been part of the scenery but had not participated in
my world. I flew and he walked. I was on familiar terms
with death and he pecked items out on a typewriter as I
do now. I was an arrogant snob. I was part of an elite. He
was an outsider. Still, I was civil; I made talk.

I believe he bought me a drink, but I am not sure. He
had done a squib on my completing my missions, he said,
and I nodded appreciatively. His face was a pasty white,
as I remember it, but I do not trust myself because I have
carried his face so long in my mind that it is the worse
for wear.

We were oppressively alone in that bar. The alcohol
had diminished me to a point below anything I had
known. My spirit had collapsed like a dishrag. Inside my
throat I could feel tears drip as from an abscess. Yet we
talked of God knows what. We talked until he said quite
suddenly, "You made it all the way. Not many of your
people stick it out."

I hope to God I did not nod my head or let my hand
shake. I know I could not speak. I think he knew I could
not speak, and that staggers me with shame thirty-five
years later. I put my drink down. That I do remember. I

do not think I looked at him. I wish now that I had, that I had seen his face clearly. I cannot tell whether he smiled or smirked or gloated or peered dully at me through his glasses. I will never know. I took my trench coat from the hook on the wall. I recall that I did everything slowly. I put on my crushed airman's hat and walked out.

That is what happened. A plethora of rationalizations followed at once and have continued for thirty-five years. The event came so suddenly upon me, so unexpectedly, that I could not think of any of the thousand witty, savage, blunt things to say or do that have leaped to mind ever since. I was caught completely off guard. I had just been tasting the joys of exclusivity at a bitter time. I had condescended to talk to this paddlefoot, this unprepossessing paper pusher. I had been in and up and he had been down and out. It had been so kind of me to talk to him. Then in the twinkling of an eye he had pulled me down and thrown me out. I walked the dark and rutted roads around Kimbolton, clutching my coat as if caught in a chill wind.

I had always acknowledged my kinship with the Jews of Europe, but it was a watery-thin intellectual nod that I sent them. I had lived in a world—social, political, sexual—where I supposed that others took my Jewishness for granted as I did and made no fuss about it. The crosses of the Klan had burned in the hills near the town I lived in as a child, but they had not referred to me. When we did not laugh at the Klan we hated it because it menaced other people. I loathed anti-Semitism in the same way because it was a scourge for other people though not for me.

Now that stupid little man had stripped the illusion from my war. It was not, then, a game which we played with death in the sky. It was not all gallantry and white contrails against the blue. It was not an aesthetic experience sanctified by an unchallengeable political cause. Hitler was not a dragon with shiny scales to be slain by a shinier knight. There were no dragons, but only savage men and women burning the flesh of other men and women. And I was a Jew with someone's spittle on my face.

I do not pretend that I was a victim of a pogrom. I agree that, living in the same century as Auschwitz, I ought not to mention my little encounter. And it would have left no mark on me if I had not been rendered so vulnerable by a false sense of security derived from the battlefield where death creates the splendid illusion of brotherhood.

None of this was clear to me as I left the bar. It has taken me thirty-five years to begin to understand that nameless PR man. He probably shrugged when I walked out, confirmed in the view that Jews are hypersensitive and unpredictable and that they can't tell a compliment from a kick in the ass.

I spent the night somehow between the officers' club and my hut. I no longer remember whether I woke when my crew left. I must have said goodbye again though I had already said as much the night before. Still, to think that I had not would shame me more than my performance at the bar. •

That afternoon Duke and I got a lift to Bedford and took the train to Surrey. Duke had been trying for months to persuade me to join him for a weekend in the cottage he shared with Madge and Bruce. He thought I would fit in. The twenty-fifth had not changed our radioman, at least not to the naked eye. He had always cultivated an impressive urbanity. I had seen it ruffled

251

at times, torn apart by exhaustion. I had seen Duke anoxic and turning blue, dangling his feet out of an open hatch 25,000 feet above Germany. I had seen him lying on the floor of a dinghy in the Channel, retching up his insides like the rest of us. Now he was cool and cocky, and I could not tell whether beneath the camouflage he nursed a spirit drained by the knowledge that for a while at least he was safe from the many possible forms of death that ride in a B-17.

Perhaps he felt as I did. Perhaps I looked as he did. I cannot tell. We were in the same situation; yet no one had remarked on how surprising it was to find one of his kind—Protestant, German American, New Yorker, ectomorph or whatever—actually completing a tour of combat. He had not been awarded that particular thorny crown to go with the DFC.

On the way down we talked again of Madge. She was more than just a lay, more than a girl to have when his wife was far away. She was a person in her own right. She knew about art and the theater, Duke said. She had read more than he had. She was smart. They went well together, he fancied. He wore her like a bright new tie or a boutonniere. He was proud of her and he very much wanted to show her off. I would like her, he thought. And Bruce was a fine fellow and a good artist. Duke pulled from his musette bag a photo of a pen-and-ink portrait Bruce had made of him. It was slick as a cigarette ad. It was unmistakably Duke, but with every feature polished, with every crease, wrinkle and ambiguity artfully dissolved. It was a Duke anyone could understand at a glance—a dashing GI, neither more nor less. Bruce was plainly an artist with a facile touch.

I acknowledged the clever likeness. Bruce was a funny Englishman, Duke said. No American would put up with such a situation. And yet why not? He and Madge had ceased to be lovers, had ceased to be man and wife, but they were friends, you see. Did I understand? Yes, he thought I would. Duke and Madge and Bruce all understood each other. They were all good friends and incidentally two of them were lovers. It was better than chasing around pubs and whorehouses, wasn't it? I told Duke again and yet again that I understood.

We changed trains somewhere in London. The suburban line ran southward, past hedgerows beyond which smoke curled from chimneys. Men in shaggy mufflers and long coats puffed on their pipes and stared at our train tooting and wailing as it went. The landscape wore a gray November blanket of the sort that makes difficult a return from battle. The dreary day would slip imperceptibly into dusk and night while droning planes, low on gas, would be calling for help all over England.

We got off at Dorking, as I recall, and there was Bruce waiting in a rakish, low-slung car of a make I did not know or don't recall. He was a very tweedy man and his mustache was a well-kept, tidy little brush. His smile was well-mannered but warm.

We drove through gently dripping lanes where, to my astonishment, roses bloomed as if it were June. A pre-Christmas chill was in the air. A light rain began to fall, pattering upon the canvas top of the car. Hayricks slipped by between the diagonal streaks of rain that swept the windows. Fog settled upon the brows of hills like a sponge or rose from the hollows like steam. It was an alien world in which I had no part. I was a passenger and a burden. I had no lines to read.

The talk of Bruce and Duke ricocheted around the little car. They may have asked me something. I'm sure Bruce did. I must have answered, because I too was a

253

properly mannered young man and I am good at that sort of thing. Words light as gossamer fended off the silence. The gentle Surrey landscape of brooks and muddy lanes on which the rain had plastered dark-brown leaves, of towns and crossroads, pubs appearing quite suddenly out of the leafy muck—all this contrasts in my mind with the springtime arrival of *Tondelayo.* Then the mud had been spring mud and *Tondelayo* had been a great galleon in a holy war.

The cottage had a fine, disheveled look, like a girl fresh from tumbling about in the hay. Wet leaves plastered everything. Water dripped from the eaves and cascaded from a broken gutter. It was a low house with small dormer windows, but one end had been altered to accommodate the lofty glass panels of a studio. The change gave the cottage a curious expression, as if it had raised one eyebrow.

Madge was a short, chipper woman with close-bobbed ash-blond hair. Her blue eyes twinkled as she kissed me on both cheeks and kissed Duke fondly on the mouth. Bruce stood there with my bag in his hand, looking like a benign brother. A fire blazed in the hearth. The table was set for dinner. I remember noting idly that it was not for four but for six.

Madge's sister was there with her husband, a major just returned from the African campaign. They came down shortly after we had shed our wet coats and while we were waiting for Bruce to come out of the kitchen with drinks. Madge's sister—what was her name?—was darker than Madge, heavier, and a bit more intense. The major was a hearty fellow, considerably older than his wife or any of us. He smiled a good deal; his wife laughed a good deal, and I cannot now remember a valid reason for either.

THE FALL OF FORTRESSES

In retrospect that dinner party seems to have been an exercise at war. This was not like the war from which I had just been banished. This was an abstract war. I knew little about the curious configurations being woven by the combatants. Words, smiles, exclamations, mock sighs and mock laughter bounced off the walls and ceiling. I swatted some words as they passed me, tossed quips and caught laughs, but vague, ominous allusions missed me as they sped by. I saw Duke's lustful eye grow glassy with the food and wine.

My own eyeballs felt hot and my lids heavy. Still we persevered through talk and food amid the clink of glasses and the hiss and crackle of the fire. I could not get a handle on what we were talking about or how we flitted from architecture to the stage to the smell of underground shelters.

I chattered into empty air and my words hit nothing as had my gun. Duke signaled to me cheerfully that somehow we would make it. And so we came to the blessed cigarette, the God-given breath after the mask is off. I tasted again the black coffee of debriefing, but the sweet tingling brandy made my eyeballs blaze.

We had come through, Duke and I, and now the formation had changed. Duke was seated on a sofa near the fireplace and I on a couch opposite. I felt the heat of the flames reach my face. Perhaps I closed my eyes, and when I opened them Madge was curled in Duke's arms. And in my own was Madge's sister.

I do not remember how she came to me, whether I had fired a flare or she had somehow seen me sinking and come to my rescue. We looked across the room, we two Americans and the two sisters. Bruce and the major were at the table. The dishes had been cleared away and they were playing chess. Feeling our eyes upon them,

they turned and waved. We smiled and cuddled closer. I
wrapped myself in the lady, luxuriated in the fullness of
her breasts beneath my hand and her open lips at mine.
This was mere dancing at the brink. I knew I would not
fall. Her breath was boozy, which made me turn away
ever so politely. I itched to have her and was happy
knowing that I would not. Close up she was not beautiful. Her words when she whispered them were slurred
and I did not understand. Still, she felt my yearning and
caressed it. Bruce and the major went on playing chess.

Would the lady's husband rise and banish me before
my time had come as I had been banished from another
heavy engagement? Would he say, "Not you. Your
people never screw."

I do not know whether these fancies whistled through
the flak holes of my mind then or whether it is only now
that I perceive them.

I do recall the moment when at last the chess game
was over and they stood and smiled by way of signal. We
disentangled ourselves from one another and rose, too. I
was saved from what I wanted. I decently subdued
myself. Madge showed me to the studio, where a bed had
been made up for me. Then she and Duke went upstairs.
They had their arms around each other and waved good
night with their free hands.

Madge's sister, looking sulky and disheveled, went up
with the major. Bruce, smiling and with brandy glass in
hand, went off to lock up. The bed had a country
dampness and I curled into myself to escape the chill. I
fell asleep at once and if I dreamed I would not now
remember. I half awoke when she came into bed.

The world was without form and void. I rolled into it
and made of it a woman's leg, smooth, rounded, veined,
answering to my touch. In flight nothing responds to one

except the gun. One smells only the gunpowder. One feels only the cold.

We did not speak. I molded out of the empty world two round breasts and a too fleshy stomach, a smooth neck, and lips which opened to a cavern where the tongue rolled. Then the world engulfed me. I could not see its face. I could not wedge a finger between it and me. The tides swallowed me. I said my last farewell to word and thought and gave myself to the green wave. Down and up again and down to *Tondelayo* wreathed in weeds. Then I mounted out of the water across the midnight sky. I shouted. I burst. I died. We covered our limp and passive nakedness with a sheet, with some whispered words—quite witless they were—and with a cigarette flaring and sinking into ash. So, without a good-night kiss to mark the end of war, we slept.

The rest, you may say, is farce, and you are right. Undeniably there were farcical aspects to my war.

Sometime later I was awakened by a hand on my shoulder. I raised my head to look about. The lady was sleeping on her side. Looming above me was the major.

I remember thinking how idiotic the situation was. I remember remarking to myself, My God, suppose I were based in Italy.

The major whispered so as not to wake his wife, "Would you come into the living room, if you don't mind, please."

I pulled on a bathrobe that had been left for me and followed him. The fire was still burning although very low. We used a bellows to fan the flame and drew closer to it. The major was in his bathrobe. I started to say there was nothing I could say, but he held up his hand and urged me not to go on like that.

He assured me it was not my fault. One might laugh,

257

but I beg you to remember that he was serious and deeply troubled and I was grateful. He tried to soothe me, assuring me repeatedly that he did not blame me. He said he had always known that if he ever found his wife in such a position, it could only be her fault. I think now he was unfair, though I don't believe I protested at the time.

We fetched a bottle of brandy and he talked about how painful it was to come home from a bloody time in Africa to find this. I agreed it was. He and I were talking cozily before the fire in a man's world from which the poor guilty lady in my bed had been excluded. I like to think now that she would have laughed at such an idea, knowing that it was she who did the inviting and the excluding. We drank another glass and felt the comradeship that thrives on a common enemy or a common desire.

He said he was leaving very early in the morning. So was I. We would go together before the others got up. Splendid, he said. Splendid, I said.

He thought it would be better if his wife woke up in the morning in his bed rather than in mine. Certainly, I said. I woke her gently. She wrapped a robe about her. Half asleep, she climbed the stairs. Her hair and breasts and belly, still warm from the bed, stirred a flutter of desire in me, perhaps in the major as well. Impervious to both of us, she did not call good night.

Thus I came away from battle, depleted and desirous. Since my last mission I had been insulted and embraced. Neither my enemy nor my lover had a name or knew mine, for the anonymity of war is as terrible and profound as that of chessmen tumbled into a box when the game is over.